ON PRAYER

ON PRAYER

ARCHIMANDRITE SOPHRONY
(SAKHAROV)

Translated from the Russian
by
ROSEMARY EDMONDS

ST VLADIMIR'S SEMINARY PRESS
CRESTWOOD, NEW YORK 10707
1998

Library of Congress Cataloging-in-Publication Data

Sofronii, Archimandrite, 1896-1993
    On prayer / Sophrony; translated from the Russian by Rosemary
Edmonds.
        p.   cm.
    Originally published: Essex: Stavropegic Monastery of St. John the
Baptist, 1996.
    Includes bibliographical references.
    ISBN 0-88141-194-9   (alk. paper)
    1. Prayer—Orthodox Eastern Church.   I. Title
BX382.S634   1998
248.3'2—dc21   98-40508
                                                                CIP

ON PRAYER

ST VLADIMIR'S SEMINARY PRESS
575 Scarsdale Rd., Crestwood, NY 10707
1-800-204-2665

ISBN 0-88141-194-9

PRINTED IN THE UNITED STATES OF AMERICA

Contents

PART I

I

PRAYER – *An ever-new Creation*

Prayer is infinite creation, far superior to any form of art or science. Through prayer we enter into communion with Him that was before all worlds. Or, to put it in another way, the life of the Self-existing God flows into us through the channel of prayer. Prayer is an act of supreme wisdom, of all-surpassing beauty and virtue. Prayer is delight for the spirit. But the circumstances accompanying this creative work are complex. Time after time we experience an eager upsurge towards God, followed repeatedly by a falling away from His Light. Time and again we are conscious of the mind's inability to rise to Him. There are moments when we feel ourselves on the verge of madness. Pain forces the cry, 'Thou didst give me Thy precept to love, which I accept with all my being, but there is no strength in me for this love. Thou Who art love, come and abide in me, and perform in me all that Thou hast enjoined, for Thy commandment exceeds my powers. My mind is too frail to comprehend Thee. My spirit cannot see into the mysteries of Thy life. I desire to do Thy will in all things but my days go by in perpetual conflict. I am tortured by the fear of losing Thee because of the evil thoughts in my heart; and this fear crucifies me. I sink. Lord, save me, as Thou didst save Peter who dared to walk on the water, to go to Thee.'[i]

At times prayer seems over-slow in bringing results, and life is so short. Instinctively we cry, 'Make haste unto me'. But

[i] cf. Matt. xiv:28–31.

9

He does not always respond at once. Like fruit on a tree, our soul is left to scorch in the sun, to endure the cold wind, the scorching wind, to die of thirst or be drowned in the rain. But if we do not let go of the hem of His garment, all will end well.

It is vital to continue in prayer for as long as we can, so that His invincible strength may penetrate and enable us to resist every destructive influence. And with the increase of this strength in us comes the joy of hope in final victory.

Prayer assuredly revives in us the divine breath which God breathed into Adam's nostrils and by virtue of which Adam 'became a living soul.'[ii.] Our spirit, regenerated by prayer, begins to marvel at the sublime mystery of being. The mind is filled with wonder. 'Being, how is it possible?' And we echo the Psalmist's praise of the wondrous works of the Lord. We apprehend the meaning of Christ's words, 'I am come that [men] might have life, and that they might have it more abundantly.'[iii.] 'More abundantly' – this is indeed so.

But again and again I find myself reflecting that life is full of paradox, like all the Gospel teaching. 'I am come to send fire on the earth; and what will I, if it be already kindled?'[iv.] All we sons of Adam must go through this heavenly flame that consumes our deathly passions. Otherwise we shall not see the fire transformed into the light of new life, for it is not light that comes first, and then fire: in our fallen state burning must precede enlightenment. Let us, therefore, bless the Lord for the consuming action of His love. We do not know altogether but we do at least know 'in part'[v.] that there is no other way for us mortals to become 'children of the resurrection,'[vi.] children of God, to reign together with

---

[ii.] Gen. ii:7.
[iii.] John x:10.
[iv.] Luke xii:49.
[v.] I Cor. xiii:9.
[vi.] Luke xx:36.

Christ, the only-begotten Son of God. However painful this re-creating may be, however it may distress and lacerate – the process, agonising as it is, in the end will be a blessed one. Erudition requires prolonged and intense labour but prayer is incalculably harder to acquire.

When the Gospels and Epistles become real for us, we see how naïve were our former notions of God and life in Him. The Wisdom that is revealed to us far surpasses man's imagining – 'Eye hath not seen, nor ear heard, neither have entered into the heart of man, the things which God hath prepared for them that love him.'[vii] Even a whisper of the Divine Spirit is glory beyond compare to all the content of life lived apart from God.

True prayer uniting us with the Most-High is nothing other than light and strength coming down to us from heaven. In its essence it transcends our plane of existence. This world contains no source of energy for prayer. If I eat well so that my body may be strong, my flesh will rebel against prayer. If I mortify the flesh by excessive fasting, for a while abstinence favours prayer but soon the body grows faint and refuses to follow the spirit. If I associate with good people, I may find moral satisfaction and acquire new psychological or intellectual experience but only very rarely will I be stimulated to prayer in depth. If I have a talent for science or the arts, my success will give rise to vanity and I shall not be able to find the deep heart,[viii] the place of spiritual prayer. If I am materially well-off and busy wielding the power associated with riches or with satisfying my aesthetic or intellectual desires, my soul does not rise up to God as we know Him through Christ. If I renounce all that I have and go into the desert, even there the opposition of the cosmic energies will paralyse my prayer. And so on, *ad infinitum*.

[vii] I Cor. ii:9.
[viii] cf. Ps. lxiv:6.

11

True prayer to the true God is contact with the Divine Spirit which prays in us. The *Spirit* gives us to know God. The *Spirit* draws our spirit to contemplation of eternity. Like grace coming down from on High the act of prayer is too much for our earthly nature and so our mortal body, incapable of rising into the spiritual sphere, resists. The intellect resists because it is incapable of containing infinity, is shaken by doubts and rejects everything that exceeds its understanding. The social environment in which I live is antagonistic to prayer – it has organised life with other aims diametrically opposed to prayer. Hostile spirits cannot endure prayer. But prayer alone can restore the created world from its fall, overcoming its stagnation and inertia, by means of a mighty effort of our spirit to follow Christ's commandments.

The struggle for prayer is not an easy one. The spirit fluctuates – sometimes prayer flows in us like a mighty river, sometimes the heart dries up. But every reduction in our prayer-strength must be as brief as possible. To pray not infrequently means telling God of our disastrous state: of our weakness and despondency, our doubts and fears, the melancholy, the despair – in brief, everything connected with our condition. To pour it all out, not seeking to express it elegantly or even in logical sequence. Often this method of approach to God turns out to be the beginning of prayer as communion.

Sometimes we shall lie afloat in a sea of Divine love, which in our imagination we interpret one-sidedly, as our love for Him. It was like that with me – I did not dare think that the infinitely great Creator of all things could heed my worthless, vile self. And I would cry, 'Oh, if only Thou couldst love me as I love Thee . . . Dost Thou not see how my heart thirsts for Thee day and night? Incline unto me. Shew me Thy countenance. Make me such as Thou dost desire to see them that Thou hast created – such as Thou, All-holy One, may receive and love . . .' I did not know what

I said.[ix.] I did not dare think that it was He Himself praying in me.

Contemplation of the holiness and humility of God astounds the soul and with deep veneration she worships Him in love. A prayer of this kind may sometimes be transformed into contemplation of the Uncreated Light.

So that we may become acquainted with His gifts, God, after being with us, leaves us for a while. This abandonment by God makes a strange impression. In my youth I was a painter. (I am afraid that the painter in me is not altogether dead.) This natural talent was part of me. I might weary, lacking the strength to work, or the inspiration, but I would always know that painting was my nature. But when God departs, He leaves a sort of blank space in the core of my being, and I do not know whether He will ever come again. He is other – different from me. He has withdrawn and I am left empty; and I feel my emptiness like a death. His coming had brought something splendid and dear to my heart that exceeded my most audacious imagining. And lo, I find myself once more in my old state which used to seem normal and satisfactory but which now appals me. I had been introduced into the house of the great King – I was His kindred – but now again I am no more than a homeless beggar.

These alternating states teach us the difference between our natural gifts and those that we receive from on High. Through prayer of repentance I was vouchsafed the first visitation; through prayer, but this time more fervent prayer, I hope to bring Him back. And indeed, He comes. Often, as a rule even, He changes the manner of His coming. Thus I am constantly being enriched by knowledge on the plane of the Spirit: now in suffering, now through joy, but I grow.

[ix.] cf. Luke ix:33.

My ability to remain for longer periods in the previously unknown sphere increases.

Keep your mind firmly fixed on God, and the moment will come when the Immortal Spirit touches the heart. Oh, this touch of the Holy of holies! There is naught on earth to compare with it – it sweeps the spirit into the realm of uncreated Being. It pierces the heart with a love unlike that which is generally understood by the word. Its light streams down on all creation, on the whole human world in its millenary manifestation. Though this love is sensed by the physical heart, by its nature it is spiritual, metaphysical.

The life-giving Divine Spirit visits us when we continue humbly open to Him. He does not violate our freedom. He envelops us with His tender warmth. He approaches us so softly that at first we may not notice Him. We must not expect God to force His way in without our consent. Far from it. He respects man, submits to Him. His love is humble – He loves us not condescendingly but tenderly, as a mother aches over her sick baby. When we open our heart to Him we have an irresistible feeling that He is our 'kin', and the soul melts in worship.

Divine love, which is the intrinsic essence of eternity, in this world cannot avoid suffering. Mellowed through ascetic striving and the visitation of grace, the heart is allowed to behold – obscurely, perhaps – Christ's love embracing the whole of creation in infinite compassion for all that exists. Now I am God's, Christ's prisoner. I recognise that I have been called out of nothing – by his nature man is nothingness. Yet in spite of this we expect compassion and respect from God. And suddenly the Almighty reveals Himself in His indescribable humility. This vision moves the soul, astonishes the mind. Involuntarily we bow before Him. And however much we try to become like Him in humility, we do not attain to Him.

Christ-like humility is an all-conquering force. It knows no degradation. It is divinely majestic. It is indescribable – what we portray in our words seems contradictory. Humility is an attribute of the God of Love, Who in His openness to all creatures meekly accepts every blow, every wound, from the hands which He fashioned.

Any vision of God places man before the necessity of self-determination in relation to Him. In essence our every action inevitably either approaches us to God or, on the contrary, distances us from Him. Hence, every venture is effected in what is termed divine fear. The soul fears not only deeds that are patently wrong but thoughts, too, that may grieve the Holy Spirit, Whom she has come to love. The distance between us and God is inexpressibly vast. We recognise that we are unworthy of the Holy of holies. The heart grieves, wearied and oppressed to see herself so destitute. We do not understand immediately that this very phenomenon signals the start of an advance towards God. The opening beatitude, 'Blessed are the poor in spirit,' organically, as it were, leads to what follows – mourning, meekness, hunger and thirst after righteousness, mercy, pureness of heart, and the first vital perception of our sonship; which inevitably entails painful conflict with the world of the passions, rupture with all who are not seeking the Kingdom of truth; persecution, abuse, vilification, and the rest. When the opposition of the Christian spirit to the spirit of this world reaches its peak, life for the follower of Christ becomes a crucifixion, however invisible the cross. It is a terrible and at the same time salutary period: through inner suffering, often linked with physical or material distress, the passions are conquered. The power of this world over us, even death itself, is defeated. We start to become like Christ crucified.

Even now, however, we must preserve humility of spirit. Experience will show that the moment we begin to feel satisfied with ourselves, instead of 'poor in spirit', the whole spiritual ladder that we have climbed collapses and 'our house is left unto us desolate.'[x] God is no longer with us. And so it will continue until the heart is humbled again and cries out to Him in pain. Through these fluctuating experiences the soul learns the secret of the ways of salvation. She fears everything that is contrary to humility. Her prayer is cleansed. Mind and heart are not attracted to anything extraneous, are desirous of naught save God. Through prayer with every fibre of his being the strength of new life flows into him who prays: the promise of further ascent, the dawn of knowledge of celestial form of being.

Our earthly existence is conditioned by time and space. But what is *time*? There are various definitions. Time is the 'place' of our meeting with the Creator. Time is the *process of the actualization of God's purpose for His creature*: 'My Father worketh hitherto, and I work.'[xi] Creation is not yet completed: 'Walk while ye have the light, lest darkness come upon you: for he that walketh in darkness knoweth not whither he goeth. While ye have light, believe in the light, that ye may be children of light.'[xii] Each of us has his allotted 'time' – brief, but enough to find salvation. The creative idea of God is realised in His creation: 'For with God nothing shall be impossible.'[xiii] On Golgotha, when He was dying, the Lord said: 'It is finished.'[xiv] Another moment will come when the same words will be uttered – the book of the Revelation tells us so: 'And the angel . . . lifted up his hand to heaven, And sware by him that liveth for ever and ever . . . that there should be time no longer.'[xv]

So long as we are in this 'body of sin' – in this world,

[x] cf. Matt. xxiii:38.
[xi] John v:17.
[xii] John xii:35–36.
[xiii] Luke i:37.
[xiv] John xix:30.
[xv] cf. Rev. x:5–6.

therefore – the ascetic battle against the 'law of sin which is in [our] members'[xvi.] must continue. Seeing ourselves unable to overcome this death by our own efforts, we despair of our salvation. Strange as it may seem, it is essential that we experience this painful state – experience it hundreds of times that it may be deeply engraved on our consciousness. This first-hand knowledge of hell is profitable for us. When we endure this torment year after year, it becomes a constant part of our spirit, a permanent sore on the body of our life. Christ, too, kept the nail-wounds from the crucifixion on His body even after His Resurrection: 'Came Jesus and stood in the midst, and saith unto them, Peace be unto you . . . And he shewed unto them his hands and his side.'[xvii.]

Experience of the torments of hell enjoins prayer for the whole human race as for ourselves.[xviii.] In spirit we translate our own individual state to universal dimensions. Thus our every experience becomes a revelation of what is happening and through the ages has always happened in the human world, and our spiritual merging with the world becomes a tangible reality.

The Lord has revealed to us the true meaning of the commandment, 'Thou shalt love thy neighbour as thyself,' in its divine boundlessness. The law of Moses envisaged this neighbour as a fellow Jew: 'Thou shalt not avenge, nor bear any grudge against the children of thy people, but thou shalt love thy neighbour as thyself.'[xix.] But Christ widened its scope to embrace all peoples for all time: 'Ye have heard that it hath been said, Thou shalt love thy neighbour, and hate thine enemy. But I say unto you, Love your enemies, bless them that curse you, do good to them that hate you, and

[xvi.] cf. Rom. vi:6; vii:23.
[xvii.] John xx:19–20.
[xviii.] cf. Matt. xxii:39.
[xix.] Lev. xix:18.

pray for them which despitefully use you, and persecute you; That ye may be the children of your Father which is in heaven.'[xx] The only-begotten Son of the heavenly Father acquainted us with this – in the Scriptures through a conversation with a 'lawyer'[xxi] and in our own life through the Holy Spirit. He Himself fulfilled the commandment in the garden of Gethsemane and on Golgotha. And we, when we enter into the spirit of this commandment, become like unto God.

Time and again I would fall into despair over my inability to live constantly in the spirit of Christ's commandments. In those bitter moments I would think: The Lord Himself said that He was not of this world.[xxii] He came down from heaven[xxiii] but I am altogether of this world, of the earth which I walk on. He, 'being in heaven', was not parted from the Father while He lived here with us; and how is it possible to be *there, where He is*? He is holy but I cannot break loose from the 'body' of the universal Adam, who in his fall turned this world into hell and placed it 'in wickedness' wherein I now lie.

What does it mean, to be not of this world? Nothing less than to be 'born from on high'. I could see no end to my distress. Abandon the quest for unity with Him? Impossible – the idea of condemning myself to separation from His Light appalled me. Woe unto me, born in sin. And who will save me from the outer darkness? Who will so transform my very nature as to make it possible for me to dwell inseparable from 'Him Who is Light, in Whom there is no darkness at all'?[xxiv]

In sin was I conceived, I was shapen in iniquity. I inherited

---

[xx] Matt. v:43–45.
[xxi] cf. Luke x:27 *et seq.*
[xxii] cf. John viii:23.
[xxiii] cf. John iii:13.
[xxiv] cf. I John i:5.

the terrible *fall of Adam*, the fall made worse by his sons down the ages; the fall which I aggravate every day of my life. And I weep and lament to see myself thus. And when my lamentations exhaust me to the point of death and I hang helpless over the abyss, then, somehow, gentle love approaches from another world, and with it – Light. This, of course, is birth from on High – not complete yet but release, nevertheless, from the power of death – the dawn of immortality. Yes, we must travel a hard road of ascetic effort for the Divine gift to grow in us. And when this wondrous gift starts to ripen and its fragrance penetrates the pores of our 'body of sin,'[xxv] the fear of death departs and we are delivered from bondage.[xxvi] And in the holy freedom thus found, we wish all men well.

Christ's love inspires compassionate prayer for all men – prayer in which soul and body take part together. Grieving over the sins of one's fellows in prayer of this kind links us with the redeeming passion of the Lord: 'Christ suffered for [our] sins, the just for the unjust . . . He suffered for us, leaving us an example, that [we] should follow his steps.'[xxvii] To be crucified together with Him is a gift of the Holy Spirit. Our heavenly Father 'favoureth' us when we grieve over our brothers who stumble. In the spirit of the commandment to love our neighbour as ourself we are bound to have pity one for another; we must establish a kind of mutual responsibility to link us all together before the face of God our Creator.

There is life-giving strength and holy joy in the soul's prayerful anguish over salvation for all people. The unusual but God-like nature of Christian life consists in combining in miraculous fashion grief and joy, depth and height, the pres-

---

[xxv] Rom. vi:6.
[xxvi] cf. Hebrews ii:15.
[xxvii] cf. I Pet. iii:18; ii:21.

ent and the future and the past in the centuries-old history of the earth. Just as the sun casts its rays in every direction, filling the expanse all around with warmth and light, so does the light and warmth of Christ-like love pierce all barriers, to lead our spirit into infinity. Where is the poet with words to express our grateful wonder at the life bestowed on us, in which dying is turned to life eternal through resurrection? 'Whosoever will lose his life for my sake shall find it.'[xxviii.] 'Verily, verily, I say unto you, Except a corn of wheat fall into the ground and die, it abideth alone: but if it die, it bringeth forth much fruit. He that loveth his life shall lose it; and he that hateth his life in this world shall keep it unto life eternal.'[xxix.]

Absorbing the revelation given to mankind from on High would appear to be a slow process, not only with humanity as a whole but with each one of us. For instance, did not the Sinaitic revelation I AM THAT I AM, take fifteen centuries before a few Israelites were able to apprehend its fulfilling by the New Testament?[xxx.] Again, twenty centuries have gone by since, in the uncreated Light on Mount Tabor and the descent afterwards of the Holy Ghost in the house in Zion, the world was given the perfect revelation of God the Holy Trinity. But how many have really assimilated this? We do not find it easy to make God's life our own. Even those who cherish the coming of Christ, the Lamb of God, cannot contain the fulness of the blessing vouchsafed to them. Those who in a transport of faith take up the cross to follow after Him suffer pain their whole life through.[xxxi.] They are fortified by the hope that when they go hence they will enter the sphere of light, where He is. 'If any man serve me, let him follow me; and where I am, there shall also

[xxviii.] Matt. xvi:25.
[xxix.] John xii:24–25.
[xxx.] cf. Matt. v:17–19.
[xxxi.] cf. Matt. xvi:24.

my servant be: if any man serve me, him will my Father honour.'[xxxii].

However fervent his faith, it will take the Christian many years of fasting and repentant prayer to 'change our vile body, that it may be fashioned like unto his glorious body.'[xxxiii]. The long process will reveal the extent of Adam's fall. The vision is not given to all in equal measure. But there are cases, however infrequent, when God's Spirit leads the repentant soul through abysses impassable to others.

Belief in the absolute God must be unshakeable. In all my years on Mt. Athos I cannot remember ever doubting. But there were times when I would weary from long prayer and exclaim, 'Oh, this is beyond my strength.' But the consequences of such flashes were invaluable.

We first of all, and above all, love Christ. The more complete the love, the more painfully we feel any violation of its harmony. When our spirit continues in prayer to the Eternal God, we lose all awareness of the duration of time and a brief instant can become a permanent state. Even where there is long experience and knowledge of the 'mechanics' of such testing, the soul not without horror detects in herself the possibility of a breach with God, and weeps bitterly, beseeching Him to heal her through and through. And He does so heal, and the heart rejoices with a new rejoicing – love which up to then seemed perfect is further enriched in quality and strength.

Earnest prayer so draws both heart and mind to the eternal that the past is forgotten. The mind has no thought for an earthly future. The soul knows but a single concern – not to lose *such* a God, and to stop being unworthy of Him. The

[xxxii]. John xii:26.
[xxxiii]. Phil. iii:21.

21

stronger our attraction to the Infinite, the slower seems our approach to Him. A wearying sensation of our worthlessness, on the one hand, and, on the other, of the inscrutable greatness of Him Whom we seek, makes any trustworthy estimate of our actual situation impossible – are we getting nearer to God or falling away? In contemplating the holiness of God man develops more quickly than he does in his ability to conform his life to the commandments. Hence the impression that the distance between us and God continually increases. In the field of science every new discovery, not being final, shows up our previous ignorance and at the same time, as it were, enlarges the area of the unknown lying before us. A mental vision of our purpose may come to us in a flash, whatever our age, but the practical realisation of what was anticipated intuitively may require a lifetime's effort, and even so there is no guarantee of success. In the field of science, as in that of the arts, there are always certain touchstones on which to base a judgment but it is otherwise with the spirit which is drawn to the Eternal.

The artist, the philosopher, the scholar may suffer torment in their creative striving, though their objective is insignificant compared with ours.

The Christian is overcome with horror when he is torn away from the Eternal where he dwelt in prayer. To see himself at the mercy of base passions cutting him off from God fills him with acute pain. Desperate prayer starts up within us in the very core of our being, in spasms, so to speak: the whole self contracts tight, like a clenched fist. Prayer becomes a wordless cry. There is nothing more distressing than to find oneself in the black pit of sin, unworthy of the Holy of holies.

Every Christian activity is inescapably bound up with ascetic striving. And love, the noblest of all activities, is the most difficult of ascetic feats. The Christian's life in essence means following Christ: 'What is [anyone else] to thee, follow thou

22

me.'[xxxiv.] Because of this, every believer will to some degree or another tread the way of the Lord — but he will not of his own strength shoulder the cross to go to Gethsemane and then Golgotha, 'for without him we can do nothing.'[xxxv.] And those to whom this fearful blessing has been granted will anticipate their resurrection. Others must rely on faith in God's mercy.

This is the heavenly Father's Providence for us: that all mortals should 'take up their cross'[xxxvi.] in order to inherit eternal life. Those who refuse will not escape slavery to the passions and will fall victim to decay of the flesh.[xxxvii.] The love for God and one's neighbour commanded of us in the Gospels involves profound suffering but this suffering is accompanied by heavenly comfort:[xxxviii.] the peace which the Lord gave to the Apostles before Golgotha quickens the soul. And when man's spirit is led into the light of the love of God our Father, all pain is forgotten and the soul knows inexpressible felicity.[xxxix.] Just as a woman 'as soon as she is delivered of the child . . . remembereth no more the anguish, for joy that a man is born into the world,'[xl.] so will the Christian rejoice even more when he is born in God for all eternity.

The believer is naturally zealous to preserve the truth of the Revelation given by the Church in, if possible, its plenitude and purity. The age-old experience of the Church has proved convincingly that every deviation from the path of the Gospel commandments distances one from the knowledge which is life everlasting.[xli.] We lack the strength to achieve the perfec-

xxxiv. cf. John xxi:22.
xxxv. cf. John xv:5.
xxxvi. cf. Matt. xvi:24.
xxxvii. cf. Gal. vi:8; Rom. viii:13.
xxxviii. cf. Mark x:29–30.
xxxix. cf. John xii:50; xvii:3.
xl. John xvi:21.
xli. John xvii:3; xii:50.

tion of the commandments but we can do our utmost, and the rest He Himself will perform. In our labours to attain to Christ-like love we begin to contemplate the height of Divine majesty which no man can approach unto and, at the same time, the immensity of His humility. The power of the commandments lies in the fact that they naturally introduce one into the infinity of Divine Being. The soul marvels before God, enraptured over His pre-eternal might, astounded at His condescension to us in His assumption of our flesh. In all things 'one is our Teacher, even Christ.'[xlii.] Without Him mankind would inevitably perish in the black gloom of its evil. Christ is 'the light of the world.'[xliii.] In Him is truth manifest and 'of his fulness have all we received, and grace for grace.'[xliv.]

God Who is humble 'resisteth the proud, and giveth grace to the humble.'[xlv.] Grace is God's life and He gives His life to them who strive for likeness to Him. 'He that shall humble himself shall be exalted.'[xlvi.] Because of this, belittling oneself to the infinitesimal is the principle of our form of asceticism, not any pretentious straining for self-aggrandizement. Our way is the way of apophatic effort through self-emptying – kenotic love – after the example of Christ Who 'humbled himself, and became obedient unto death, even the death of the cross.'[xlvii.] The more thoroughly we 'make ourselves of no reputation,' the more radically shall we be cleansed from the consequences of the prideful fall of our forefather Adam. And when our heart becomes 'pure,'[xlviii.] then the Father, the Son and the Holy Spirit come to dwell in us, and we are

[xlii.] cf. Matt. xxiii:8.
[xliii.] John viii:12.
[xliv.] John i:16–17.
[xlv.] I Pet. v:5.
[xlvi.] Matt. xxiii:12.
[xlvii.] cf. Phil. ii:5–9.
[xlviii.] Matt. v:8.

led into the 'kingdom which cannot be moved'[xlix.] where infinite majesty merges with infinite humility and meekness.

The very incarnation of God the Word is also a self-emptying, ontologically natural to divine love. The Father empties Himself of all things in the birth of the Son. And the Son appropriates nothing to Himself but gives all things to the Father. Our self-emptying means renouncing all that we hold dear on earth in fulfilment of the commandment, 'If any man will come after me, let him deny himself, and take up his cross . . . For whosoever will save his life shall lose it; and whosoever will lose his life for my sake shall find it.'[l.] 'So likewise, whosoever he be of you that forsaketh not all that he hath, he cannot be my disciple.'[li.]

And that is the way of the living God.

'A certain lawyer . . . tempted Jesus, saying, Master, what shall I do to inherit eternal life? Jesus said unto him, What is written in the law? how readest thou? And he answering said, Thou shalt love the Lord thy God with all thy heart, and with all thy soul, and with all thy strength, and with all thy mind; and thy neighbour as thyself. And Jesus said unto him, Thou hast answered right: this do, and thou shalt live' (an eternal life in God).[lii.] To the lawyer's query, 'And who is my neighbour?' the Lord answered with the parable of the good Samaritan, the essential meaning of which at that time lay in the commandment: 'Love ye your enemies, and do good . . . hoping for nothing again; and your reward shall be great, and ye shall be the children of the Highest.'[liii.]

Staretz Silouan described the state of our spirit when grace is given us from on High to love our enemies, as experience

[xlix.] Heb. xii:28.
[l.] Matt. xvi:24–25.
[li.] Luke xiv:33.
[lii.] cf. Luke x:25–37.
[liii.] Luke vi:35.

of divine eternity while we are still within the confines of this life. He both said and wrote, 'The man who does not love his enemies has not yet come to know God as we ought to know Him.'

I would venture to add, in explanation of this grace, that he who is illumined by the uncreated Light of the Holy Spirit shining within him, and so lives the passing 'from death to life everlasting', naturally pities all those who lack this blessing. Being outside death, he is liberated from all fear of adversity and knows the Father's thought for him: 'Son, thou art ever with me, and all that I have is thine.'[liv.] And if all that the Father has is given to us, it is only natural for the soul to 'make merry, and be glad' when the brother that was dead quickens to imperishable glory in the Kingdom of the living God.[lv.]

To be a Christian means believing in the resurrection of the dead; hoping for the 'adoption of sons'[lvi.] by the heavenly Father; receiving the divine image of being; becoming through the gift of the Father's love what He Himself is by His nature – a god. These things hath our Father promised to those who believe in Christ Jesus as the only-begotten Son of one substance with the Father. It is a great sin to belittle the revelation given to us in the Holy Spirit concerning Man, on how Man was conceived by God before the creation of the visible world. Punishment for this sin – unbelief in the Resurrection – bears a particular stamp: it is our own self-condemnation – we refuse the gift of our Creator. Why do we? First and foremost, because the Father's gift has to be acquired at the cost of much labour, much suffering. This is an extraordinarily profound theme – who is capable of explaining it to people of varying levels of knowledge and understanding? And who can properly por-

[liv.] Luke xv:31.
[lv.] cf. Luke xv:32.
[lvi.] Gal. iv:5.

tray the equally particular delight of our spirit when the Light of Divinity reveals to us the all-wise ways of the living God?

But how are we to believe in the possibility of resurrection for all eternity after our death in the body? Everything that we experience seems to be connected expressly with this body, with its perceptions. Even our thinking we see as the movement of a kind of energy in our physical brain and heart. Not everyone has been given the experience of the state of prayer when the spirit is free from material fetters, from the conditions of time and space. Far from it. Yet we believe in science with a naïve faith, in spite of its obvious relativity. To master its latest achievements we submit from our earliest years to decades of not always easy effort. In its highest forms spiritual action goes immeasurably farther than any human science but in its early stages it is simple and even joyous. Let me try to explain the real reason for people's refusal to follow Christ – the *Truth*.

'If Christ be preached that he rose from the dead, how say some among you that there is no resurrection of the dead? But if there be no resurrection of the dead, then is Christ not risen: And if Christ be not risen, then is our preaching vain, and your faith is also vain . . . If in this life only we have hope in Christ, we are *of all men most miserable . . .* And why stand we in jeopardy every hour? I [Paul] *die daily* . . .'[lvii.]

'And James and John, the sons of Zebedee, come unto him, saying, Master, we would that thou shouldest do for us whatsoever we shall desire. And he said unto them, What would ye that I should do for you? They said unto him, Grant unto us that we may sit, one on thy right hand, and the other on thy left hand, in thy glory. But Jesus said unto them, Ye know not what ye ask: can ye drink of the cup that I drink of? and be baptized with the baptism that I am

[lvii.] I Cor. xv: 12–14, 19, 30, 31.

27

baptized with? And they said unto him, We can. And Jesus said unto them, Ye shall indeed drink of the cup that I drink of; and with the baptism that I am baptized withal shall ye be baptized.'[lviii.]

'Jesus was withdrawn from them about a stone's cast, and kneeled down, and prayed, Saying, Father, if thou be willing, remove this cup from me . . . And being in an agony he prayed more earnestly: and his sweat was as it were great drops of blood falling down to the ground.'[lix.]

What exactly is this 'cup' of Christ's? The core of the mystery is hidden from us. In our attempt to follow Christ by keeping His commandments we inevitably and constantly drink of a cup but the cup that Christ was thinking of and which He drank 'at that hour' we do not fully understand. Nevertheless, something similar certainly happens with us, as He Himself said: 'Ye shall indeed drink of the cup that I drink of.'[lx.] Mysterious is this 'cup' of Christ's but our cup, too, is hidden from alien eyes.

'If in this life only we have hope in Christ, *we are of all men most miserable,*' said St. Paul.[lxi.] He is right, indeed. But what is it that makes this blessed 'misery' inexplicable to those who have not followed Christ? Is it not because all the reactions of the Christian spirit to everything going on around us are profoundly different from, and often diametrically opposed to, those of the children of this world? For instance – Judas departed from the upper chamber in order to betray the Lord, and at that very moment His mouth was opened and He said, 'Now is the Son of man glorified, and God is glorified in him.'[lxii.] And so it is all through the Gospel – we observe the Lord living on another plane of being, where every refraction passes through a different kind of

[lviii.] Mark x:35–39.
[lix.] cf. Luke xxii:41–42 and 44.
[lx.] Mark x:39.
[lxi.] I Cor. xv:19.
[lxii.] John xiii:31.

prism. And he who would know, if only in part, of this mystery must shoulder his cross and commit himself entirely to the will of the heavenly Father. There is no other way. And still there is no end to the conflict between Christ and this world.

I love and feel profound gratitude to the Church in whose bosom the Divinity of Jesus Christ and His image were revealed to me. We can see this 'image' in a diminished form in the lives of individual people, as we can in our own. Its consummation belongs to the world to come but the rare approximations through the centuries also entrance the soul. It is normal for the Christian to long to become like the Lord; to embrace the world with love as He embraced it; like Him not to have enemies – that is, be free from the hell of hatred towards anyone at all, in accordance with His command: 'But I say unto you, Love your enemies, bless them that curse you, do good to them that hate you, and pray for them which despitefully use you, and persecute you; That ye may be the children of your Father which is in heaven.'[lxiii.] But none of the sons of Adam can live thus of his own strength. It can only be if the Holy Spirit charges the heart of man with His inherent eternity. Without Him we cannot keep God's commandments.[lxiv.]

Yes, the longing to resemble Christ is natural to the Christian. But 'strait is the gate, and narrow is the way, which leadeth unto [this divine] life.'[lxv.] To discard the skin that it no longer needs, the snake wriggles through narrow crevices. So the man who would be saved must go through very 'strait gates' in order to rid himself of the 'coats of skins' with which he was clothed after the Fall.[lxvi.]

[lxiii.] Matt. v:44–45.
[lxiv.] cf. John xv:5.
[lxv.] Matt. vii:14.
[lxvi.] cf. Gen. iii:21.

He Who said, 'I am the way, the truth, and the life,' gave us commandments like this one: 'If any man come to me, and hate not his father, and mother, and wife, and children, and brethren, and sisters, yea, and his own life also, he cannot be my disciple.'[lxvii.] These words show us WHO this is.[lxviii.] If Christ in His *hypostatic* being were not of one substance with the Father and the Holy Spirit; if he were not God, Who appeared to us in our flesh, but only a created being like us, ontologically it would not have been possible for such ideas to occur to Him. If Jesus Christ were not God this commandment would be enough to render unacceptable all the rest of the Gospel. The Church's two thousand years' experience confirms indisputably that 'great is the mystery of godliness: God was manifest in the flesh, justified in the Spirit.'[lxix.] Apprehended by faith as the unoriginate Lord, Christ becomes the Light of eternity for us, and His words reveal to us the unimaginable depths of Divine Being.

God in His unfathomable providence vouchsafed that I should meet with Silouan, chosen child of the Highest.[lxx.] Observing Silouan's ascetic striving, reverently listening to his teaching, even I, the most worthless of men, was able to glimpse the secret of the road to salvation. Now, towards the end of my days, I venture to discuss matters hitherto jealously concealed. I speak here within the limits and after the manner in which it has been given to me to live God.

In other chapters I shall write of my terrible stumbling – of my wilful and proud estrangement from the revelation given to us in Christ. But the Father – blessed be His Name world without end – showed me His Son in the Light that never sets, and thus made me so forcefully perceive my sin – I had disdained God – that for long years I wept, prostrate,

[lxvii.] Luke xiv:26–27; 33; cf. Matt. xvi:24–25.
[lxviii.] cf. Matt. xxi:10.
[lxix.] I Tim. iii:16.
[lxx.] cf. Luke vi:35.

in despair over my wickedness. I recognised my behaviour in departing from God in all its abomination, and felt bitter shame. I became abhorrent to myself, and my self-contempt found a fellow-traveller − self-hatred. I cannot say that I hated my father or my mother, my family or my friends. It was enough for me to detest myself, I somehow did not even think about anyone else. My longing for God caused me intolerable pain − such pain that I lost all awareness of the material world, as I sojourned alone with Him. I do not know whether the Lord altogether forgave me my sin but I could not forgive myself for what I had done. Through my personal tragedy I lived the tragedy of our forefather Adam − the heritage handed down from generation to generation of the inhabitants of the earth. Through this channel prayer came to me for all the world.

I lived spontaneously, without analysing my experiences. I was not in the habit of observing myself. I simply gave myself over to the powerful current of God's strength flowing into me. But I did not presume to think that He Himself was praying in me − I felt as if this life force were my own. And it was only when my agony of repentance disappeared that I realised that Christ had given me the blessedness of drawing near to Him.

Only God the Giver of all good things is really aware of the extent to which He gave me to know His love. Thanks to Staretz Silouan, my eyes, too, were opened and I understood that Christ's commandment to love Him to the point of self-hatred is a revelation of the law of Divine Love − the love with which He loved us.

If the commandments to love God with all our strength, and our neighbour as ourself originated from some prophet or other, a mortal being like the rest of us, it would lack the meaning we seek. But we have them from God the Creator of all that is, and we know that His commandments are God's Self-revelation for us. We can only keep them by 'putting off the old man, and putting on the new'[lxxi.] which is Christ the Lord from heaven.[lxxii.]

When we live in the spirit of the Gospel prescripts we are already divinised, because the power of eternal life permeates us. We are bidden to love. The property of love is to unite in very being. The fulness of love makes us love to the point of forgetfulness of self. To forgetfulness — that is, to hate for oneself.

Eternal glory be to God our Saviour for ever and ever.

[lxxi.] cf. Col. iii:9; Eph. iv:24.
[lxxii.] cf. I Cor. xv:47.

II

PRAYER – *The Way to Knowledge*

'O God, thou knowest my foolishness; and my sins are not hid from thee'[i] . . . Now I live in abject fashion but Thou, O Christ, dost call me to believe and accept the revelation that the Father loves us as He loves Thee, His only-begotten Son. 'For the Father himself loveth you, because ye have loved me . . . Neither pray I for these alone, but for them also which shall believe on me through their word; That they all may be one; as thou, Father, art in me, and I in thee, that they also may be one in us: that the world may believe that thou hast sent me . . . and hast loved them, as thou hast loved me.'[ii]

Faith in Christ makes us immeasurably bold. It was not without cause that St. Paul said, 'The foolishness of God is wiser than men.' What seems utter foolishness to the 'fleshly mind' is wisdom and strength, life and light to the believer.[iii]

But if venturing to be a Christian is an act beyond man's capacity, how can I speak of myself? From my earliest years I was aware of my nothingness. I lacked confidence even with people. And yet a measure of Light did irradiate me, and I believed in Christ-God. Belief in Him brought a more abundant outpouring of Light and my faith was intensified by new knowledge.

However much of a 'nonentity' I really was, the Uncreated Light appeared to me precisely because of my faith in Christ.

[i] Ps. lxix:5.
[ii] John xvi:27; xvii:20–23.
[iii] cf. I Cor. i:18–30; Col. ii:18.

My mind overcame the barrier of reason which cannot apprehend that the Persona-Hypostasis possesses all-comprehensive knowledge, so much so that nothing in the whole of cosmic being is hid from Him. 'Not a sparrow shall fall on the ground without [the will of] your Father . . . The very hairs of your head are all numbered . . . For there is nothing covered, that shall not be revealed; and hid that shall not be known.'[iv] Neither is there any creature that is not manifest in his sight: but all things are naked and opened unto the eyes of him with whom we have to do.'[v]

My relations with God are of an exclusively personal nature. Unless the connection is a personal one, there can be no conception of sin, no love between man and God, no existential knowledge of God; and all is swallowed up by death, obliterated in very literal non-existence.

What I want to write of now happened over half a century ago. It was a period of strain. Much – practically everything – was a puzzle to me. And life is so short! And God so immeasurably great and far off! Who will show me the straight way to Him, prevent me from wasting time on alien paths? Of course I sought such a guide, or guides – preceptors who might help me. But the fact that I was caught up by a hitherto-unknown force in the form of prayer which stayed with me day and night naturally made prayer my constant prop. And there were times when prayer, so I believe, brought enlightenment from God. I will cite an instance or two which made their mark on me and became the foundation stones of my life.

Unable to glimpse the divine truth in the destinies of mankind, of people in general, and tormented by my own dark ignorance, I was like a small, utterly helpless child. Feeling that there was something that I had to understand, I writhed impatiently and looked to God for help. And the

[iv] cf. Matt. x:29–30, 26.
[v] Heb. iv:13.

34

Lord took pity on my ignorance and was not angry at my temerity but like a mother had compassion on me and was quick to respond. And this not once but over and over again. In like manner He had handled Job who suffered so much and protested so stormily.

I remember one such happening, which occurred in France, in the early twenties – before my departure to Mt. Athos in 1925. I wept and prayed to God: 'Find a way to save the world – to save all of us, we are all defiled and cruel.' I would pray with particular fervour for the 'little ones', the poor and oppressed. Towards morning, with my strength waning, my prayer would be disturbed by the thought that if *I* grieve for mankind with all my heart, how is it that God can look on indifferently at the pain and torment of millions of beings whom He Himself had created? Why does He allow the innumerable instances of brute force in the world? And I would turn to Him with the insane challenge, 'Where art Thou?' And in my heart I heard: 'Was it you who was crucified for them?' . . . The gentle words uttered by the Spirit shook me to the core – He Who was crucified had answered me as God.

A brief response, but the divine word introduces a new, especial sense of being into the soul. The heart experiences a surge of light-bearing life. The mind suddenly grasps hitherto concealed meanings. Contact with His creative energy recreates us. Cognition that comes in this fashion is not the same as philosophical intellection: together with perception of the realities of the spiritual plane man's whole being takes on another form of life – similar, perhaps, to the first-created. This existential knowledge of God dissolves into a current of prayerful love for Him.

God answered me in a few words but words which contain an inexpressibly profound and vast revelation. Let me try to find an analogy accessible to our rational formation. In our fallen state we are separated from God by a thin veil – invisible and at the same time impenetrable. And in an unforeseen way, at a sign from God, a tiny split appears in this veil. Putting an eye to the split, we see not only what we had prayed about but wide horizons in the same perspective.

If our eye be 'single',[vi] and we keep it fixed on the vision we have been given, it will behold and be conscious of the infinity of the luminous Kingdom. And then not just our enquiry but a whole range of other related questions will find the satisfactory response. In the Divine eternity all 'parallels' are knotted together in a ball, as are all divergent rays.

Then I started to ponder – if God be such as the crucified Christ made clear, then it is we, and we only, who are guilty of all the evil throughout the history of mankind. God manifested Himself in our flesh. Humility is a natural attribute of His love. Divine humility, we may adumbrate as a readiness to accept all and every wound at the hands of creatures created by Him. And, of course, this humility is indescribable. But we did not just reject Him – we put Him to what was in our eyes a shameful death. And I saw in spirit that it was not absence of compassion on God's part that was the cause of human misery but, only and entirely, man's abuse of the gift of freedom – 'All things are lawful unto me, but all things are not expedient'[vii] – which even our fall did not deprive us of.

He was victorious in my dispute with him. At first I was all bitter shame for my mad pride – as though I were more compassionate than God! Shame led to abject self-condemnation. Then joy took over – not only had the Lord not condemned me for my audacity but He had even poured rich blessing on my head. Later I came to understand that my very prayer had been God's action in me.

To continue, and describe the spiritual experience accorded to me is not a simple task. I lived on the borders of two worlds, torn between the visible and the invisible –

[vi] cf. Matt. vi:22.
[vii] I Cor. vi:12.

between the world of the mind and the realm of heaven. In saying that I was set on the border between two worlds, I want to show that what happened to me transcended me: the initiative was not mine but that of the living God into Whose sacred hands I had fallen.[viii] My spirit, although I suffered, wondered in amazement before God.

Experience showed me how inert our nature is in sin. Even such outpourings to God as I have cited do not instantly restore our wayward nature. Under the constantly increasing pressure of the external events of our century, which looked more and more menacing, again and again I found myself in conflict with God. Now I realise that although superficially I was leading an apparently blameless life, in my depths – spiritually – I was, and am, darkness itself.

More than once my prayer – if such it could be called – was inadmissibly audacious. Seeing all over the world the nightmare of principalities and powers crushing the little man, though 'all we are brethren,'[ix] I would protest bitterly: 'If Thou didst create all things; if without Thee "was not any thing made that was made,"[x] then all these foul criminals who are prepared to shed the blood of millions for the perverted satisfaction of lording it for a few days over us poor wretches – it is not they who are indictable, they are not responsible.'

It was a time of sore trial. I was on the edge of despair, foul despair. I saw no way out. And again the Lord visited me, and my thoughts took another turning. 'The Father sent His Son to save the world; but even Him they slew. But He rose, the Conqueror of death, and as the King of all eternity will "minister judgment to the people in uprightness." '[xi]

So then where are we? The question of good and evil is not resolved on the earthly plane. Those who have gone like

---

[viii] cf. Heb. x:31.
[ix] cf. Matt. xxiii:8.
[x] John i:3.
[xi] Ps. ix:8.

sheep to the slaughter, 'resisting not evil,'[xii] will become like the Son of the Father[xiii] and will rise again with Him in glory everlasting.[xiv]

Woe is me that for a second time I fought with God in the same perspective. But my whole life continued to be preoccupied with seeking a categorical solution to the question which was to become a cardinal one for all Christianity – how react to the persecution perpetrated by the princes of this world? The Lord granted me the grace to muse after this fashion: St. Peter in the garden of Gethsemane reacted in a normal way. But Christ said to him, 'Put up thy sword into the sheath: the cup *which my Father hath given me*, shall I not drink it?'[xv]

This was how through prayer I learned precepts directly from on High. This was how the meaning was revealed to me of the Epistle to the Ephesians[xvi] concerning the breadth, and length, and depth, and height of the Divine purpose for us. Our earthly life is in effect no more than a brief moment given to us by the Good Father in order that we may 'know the [kenotic] love of Christ, which passeth knowledge, that we may be filled with *all the fulness of God.*' Here we hang on our cross, be it still an invisible one; but only thus are the greatness of man and the searchless depths of Divine Being made manifest. There are no words to tell of the God-sent richness of the way of the cross.

God is indivisible in Himself. When He comes, He comes *wholly*, as He is in His eternal Being. We do not contain Him. He reveals Himself to us at the 'point' where we knock: 'Knock, and it shall be opened unto you.'[xvii] He speaks in brief *dicta* but life is not long enough to uncover their full content. Reverently we sense His Fatherhood, His

---

[xii] cf. Matt. v:39.
[xiii] cf. Isa. liii:7.
[xiv] cf. Col. iii:1–4.
[xv] cf. Matt. xvi:22–23; John xviii:10–11.
[xvi] cf. Chapter iii.
[xvii] Luke xi:9.

clemency. We see that He hungers to communicate to us His eternal life: to have us attain the perfection of His Son, Who is the equal mould of the Father. Incomprehensible is His design for us. From 'nothing' He creates gods like Himself. And our whole being bows before Him – not in dread before the stern Master but in humble love for the Father.

The Lord preserved me from ties which it would have been difficult to break. And so when I needed freedom from all responsibility for other lives, I had it. I thanked God for this His care for me. I knew that if I died, no one would suffer any loss. I was immensely fortunate – I could risk anything, even death. All my attention was concentrated within, on my inner self, and continued so for years on end. Prayer varied in form and strength, not always attracting me with equal force; but at times I was insatiable. And if then (still in France, before my departure for Mt. Athos) I had wanted to call a halt, I could not have done so. In those blessed days I was both the most wretched creature on earth and the most utterly blessed.

Sometimes an invisible fire touched the top of my head and flashed through my body to my feet, and fervent prayer for the world accompanied by much weeping would possess me for hours on end.

For the most part I would pray on my knees, my forehead pressed to the floor. When my body became exhausted I would fall asleep but my sub-conscious self continued in prayer and I was not aware of being asleep. Only when I woke did I realise that my body had been sleeping because it was not always in the position in which I had been praying.

Twice, or perhaps three times, in the streets of Paris I lost, because of prayer, all sense of the material world around me. I would arrive at my destination all right. I regret, to a certain extent, that there was no eye-witness with me who could have described my behaviour on such occasions.

Once (in Paris) I was at a reception for a famous poet who was reading his verse. It was a gathering of the élite. Everything was perfectly organised from the social point of view. I left at midnight. On the way home I wondered how this manifestation of one of the noblest forms of human creativity could be co-related to prayer. Entering my room, I began to pray, 'O Holy God, Holy and Strong, Holy and Immortal . . .' – and lo, a fine flame gently flickered over the surface of my face and chest, light as a breath of air, yet not consonant with the Divine Spirit.

Inside myself I was torn between art and prayer. After a stubborn, long-drawn-out contest prayer won. Subsequently, in the Theological Institute now, prayer did not help me to concentrate my attention on the subject being taught. I had to struggle with these peculiar obstacles which are invaluable *per se*. It was a great help to me at the Institute that I was given a room to myself over the professors' quarters where I could pray in my usual attitude. Nevertheless, despite all my interest in the life and history of the Church my spiritual need to dwell in prayer was impaired, and I departed for Mt. Athos.

There, on the Holy Mountain, my life found its right track. Almost every day after the Liturgy I knew a feeling of Easter joy. And, strange as it may seem, my constant prayer like some volcanic eruption proceeded from the profound despair that had taken over my heart. Two seemingly totally incompatible states met together in me. I am recording facts. I did not understand myself what was happening to me. Outwardly I was no less fortunate than most people.

Later, things became clear to me: The Lord had granted me the grace of repentance.[xviii] Yes, it was a grace. The moment despair slackened, prayer cooled off and death would invade my heart. Through repentance, my being expanded until in spirit I touched upon both hell and the Kingdom. With the First World War in 1914 news of thousands of deaths on the various fronts, as I saw it, plunged the whole of cosmic being into an impenetrable fog of absurdity. I could not accept either death or the absurdity. I found myself

[xviii] cf. Luke xxiv:47.

half thinking, half feeling that everything I knew, everything I loved, that gave me life and inspired me – absolutely everything, even God Himself – would die if I ceased to exist. It was a potent experience: man, *qua persona*, could become a repository of all that exists.

I was living in two worlds. One I apprehended through sight, hearing and the rest of my physical faculties. In the other world I was spirit only – all listener, all expectation. I tried hard to see – but saw with other eyes. These two widely distinct worlds were not divided in prayer. In the daytime prayer flowed in the tangible world. But at night prayer carried me into an immaterial, spiritual sphere – I do not know how to label the infinity that embraced me. When I read the Gospels all the words were familiar but what lay behind each of them in the very Being of God, I could not comprehend. One point was strikingly clear to me – everything was to be found in Christ, Son of God, and only in Him. And to Him I prayed. I prayed likewise to the Father, that the Spirit of Truth proceeding from Him might descend even unto me, to guide me into all truth.[xix] My search for the *Deus Absconditus* found many echoes in the Old Testament which responded to my case, many words that expressed my needs. I sympathised with Job's protests, with the groans of the prophets who were born before Christ. I gleaned inspiration for prayer from the Psalms. But I only really learned from the New Testament, my touchstone for all things, whatever their origin. My thirst to know God was unquenchable – however much I prayed, however deeply I yearned, my spirit was never satisfied. Such was my 'cup' on Mt. Athos. Grief and joy flowed into it, diluting each other. I saw no way clear before me – I was at a complete loss, and filled with pain. But it was this very atmosphere of spiritual pain that gave birth to an understanding of the greatness of man. And is not this sacred pain one of the channels through which the Supreme God communicates

[xix] cf. John xvi:26, 13.

with His creature, gradually giving him knowledge not only of created-cosmic being but of Him Himself?

When the Living God appeared to Blessed Staretz Silouan it was given to the Staretz to know with his whole being the 'inexpressible humility of God'. The Staretz' teaching was effectual for many, as even for me. Thanks to him I saw clearly that the fall into pride lay at the root of all the tragedies of mankind. Pride is the very essence of hell, a hell of satanic depths. As I write, I remember with bitter shame Satan once tempting me with the thought – this was long before I met the Staretz – 'Why is Christ the only-begotten, and not I?' Merely a flash – but the flames of hell scorched my heart. God saved me. Furthermore, I caught a glimpse of the mystery of all falls.

God saved me and my love for Him grew deeper. But I remained for ever conscious that no one finds salvation of his own strength. No one can be sure that his wicked thought will not possess him for all eternity. The Lord emerged from the desert triumphant over all the temptations of the evil spirit.[xx]

God saved me. But I was horror-stricken at the very fact that such ideas could occur to me. 'There is no hope of salvation for me,' I would think. 'God could not possibly accept me for eternity, the way I am.[xxi] And besides, wouldn't it be too uncomfortable for me to be with Him, if it means for ever struggling with the passions?'

The Divine Providence was astonishingly attentive to me: at the requisite moment the Lord suffered me to meet and talk with Staretz Silouan. Thanks to the Staretz there came a definitive turning-point in my inner life. He explained to me about 'keeping my mind in hell and not despairing'. My gratitude to him was profound. I realised that in the past the Lord had led me in the same perspective but I had been too

[xx] cf. Matt. iv:1–11.
[xxi] cf. John xvii:21–23.

dense to comprehend. Thanks to the Staretz, I began to be acquainted with the ways of the Lord, and in fear and trembling I bless His Name.

'If a man love me, he will keep my words' . . . 'He that hath my commandments, and keepeth them, he it is that loveth me' . . . 'He that loveth me not keepeth not my sayings' . . . 'He that rejecteth me . . . hath one that judgeth him: the word that I have spoken, the same shall judge him in the last day.'[xxii.]

On Mt. Athos, too, as had happened before I became a monk, my prayer was more than once interrupted by rebellious thoughts. For instance, on one occasion, submitting myself to the agonising judgment of the Lord's word and feeling utter inability to abide in the spirit of His commandments, however hard I tried, I madly addressed God: 'Thou hast no right to judge me. To have the right to judge me, Thou must put Thyself in my place . . . Thou art infinite in the strength of eternal Being, while I am a creature-thing no more than a worm.' My prayer was impertinent. But all the same, the answer came, 'The Father judgeth no man, but hath committed all judgment unto the Son . . . because he is the Son of man.'[xxiii.] Until then I had not understood the words in that sense. I was abashed. I felt ashamed – I had always lived in circumstances considerably easier than those in which Christ passed His earthly life. He did indeed have the right to judge the whole world. There is no one whose sufferings have surpassed His suffering. Outwardly, many have endured, and to this day endure, terrible torture in captivity everywhere but qualitively His hell, 'the hell of love', is more agonising than every other.

'The Father . . . hath committed all judgment unto the Son, because He is the Son of man.' But what is this judgment

---

[xxii.] John xiv:23, 21, 24; xii:48.
[xxiii.] John v:22, 27.

based on? On the fact that He showed that it is possible for man to keep the Father's commandments in all circumstances to be met with in this world. It is no excuse for me to plead 'human' weakness. Similarly, those who followed Christ on earth received the right together with Him to judge the world: 'Do ye not know that the saints shall judge the world?'[xxiv] St. Peter said unto the Lord, 'Behold, we have forsaken all, and followed thee; what shall we have therefore? And Jesus said unto them, Verily I say unto you, That ye which have followed me, in the regeneration when the Son of man shall sit in the throne of his glory, ye also shall sit upon twelve thrones, judging the twelve tribes of Israel.'[xxv]

Why is this so? We find the answer in the Gospel: (1) The parents of the man who was born blind feared the Jews, who declared that 'if any man did confess that he was Christ,' (that is, the Messiah) 'he should be put out of the synagogue'[xxvi] . . . and (2) 'Among the chief rulers also many believed on him; but . . . they did not confess him, lest they should be put out of the synagogue.'[xxvii] 'They shall put you out of the synagogues: yea, the time cometh, that whosoever killeth you will think that he doeth God service.'[xxviii] It was no small risk in those days to expose oneself to social ostracism. The disciples, however, resolved to follow Him; hence their 'right' to judge those who denied Him.

'The Father himself loveth you, because ye have loved me.'[xxix] It is not without sadness that I remember the years of my youth when the meaning of these sacred words was hidden from me. I muse to myself that for centuries the message has come down from heaven in one form or another without evoking adequate response in our hearts, in our thinking which has grown indifferent to the things of the

[xxiv] I Cor. vi:2.
[xxv] Matt. xix: 27–28.
[xxvi] John ix:22, 34.
[xxvii] John xii:42.
[xxviii] John xvi:2.
[xxix] John xvi:27.

44

Divine world. And yet there have been not a few instants when words from on High struck the hearts of men like thunder, and like lightning illumined their conscience. The message descended on our earth from the mystic Kingdom like a saving revelation of the ineffable wisdom of the Heavenly Father, of His love for us, of the great mystery of His Being.

Down the ages the sacred words have been repeated without proper attention and, possibly because of this, they have lost their primordial might – the might which they first had for the prophets, apostles and saints. Will other ways be found to express the profound purport of the knowledge that we have been given of the great God? Our love for Him would wish to express itself with such lively energy that Time, the destroyer of all things, could not diminish.

We watch the inexpressibly wonderful miracle of the creation of the world, of the creation of gods,[xxx] which is not yet complete.[xxxi] The completion is promised for the world to come. But even now, too, when the Uncreated Light descends on us, this spiritual process rouses delight in the depths of our spirit, raises our thoughts to the Kingdom[xxxii] prepared for us.

Gaining this Kingdom of the Father's love entails much suffering.[xxxiii] The heart is stricken with pain when it realises the loss suffered by man. I am speaking of spiritual, metaphysical pain, and would wish my reader to understand me rightly. There is always a certain fluidity in our language: the words are the same but every new experience alters the content of ideas and the meaning they express.

The pain that the Christian ascetic feels in his heart is not a pathological symptom: it occurs 'organically', having its origin in compassionate love. One does not cultivate it –

[xxx] cf. John x:34; Ps. lxxxii:6.
[xxxi] cf. John v:17.
[xxxii] cf. Matt. xxv:34.
[xxxiii] cf. Matt. xi:12; xxv:34.

that would be to lean towards an unhealthy *dolour*. It is not the result of some psychological conflict or unsatisfied passion. It is of a quite different nature. Our birth into eternity in God entails much labour. The prophet Isaiah put it splendidly: 'And as a woman in travail draws nigh to be delivered, and cries out in her pain; so have we been to thy beloved. We have conceived, O Lord, because of thy fear, and have been in pain, and have brought forth the breath of thy salvation, which we have wrought upon the earth.' (I quote from the *Septuagint* – Isaiah chapter 26: verses 17, 18 – the text used in the Orthodox Church and justified by the millenary experience of the ascetic Fathers.) St. Paul wrote to the Galatians, 'My little children, of whom I travail in birth again, until Christ be formed in you.'[xxxiv] I could cite many more such instances from the Scriptures and the works of the Fathers.

Our spirit is aching but this pain affects the whole man – the heart, the body. The whole man suffers in the presence of the eternal God but these sufferings do not destroy: they quicken us. The torments of the spirit are by their essence metaphysical. They belong to the luminous realm of immortality. Through them we rise beyond the frontiers of matter, into the world of uncreated Light.

It is not enough to be convinced in one's mind of the Divinity of Christ in order to comprehend all things properly. We must make the maximum effort to live according to His word. Having perceived through this ascetic effort the cosmic dimensions of our fall, we must follow up with a prolonged prayer of repentance. Only then will it be given to us to live as Christ lived – humbling ourselves and becoming 'obedient unto death.'[xxxv] Only after that shall we become worthy of receiving 'power from on high'[xxxvi] or 'cloven tongues like

[xxxiv] Gal. iv:19.
[xxxv] cf. Phil. ii:6 *et seq*.
[xxxvi] Luke xxiv:49.

as of fire'^{xxxvii.} or the light of the Transfiguration on Mount Tabor. Then will the true meaning of the Gospel 'glad tidings' be clear to us.

The seven years that I spent 'in the desert' were the most favourable time for prayer. I remember starting the Lord's Prayer, 'Our Father,' and my soul swooned in blissful awe. I could not go on. My mind stopped. Everything in me fell silent. And now I find it sad to be writing about the marvel that I have lost. Only once did it happen to me with such force. Perhaps because the fiery touch of the Divine glory is too much for our physical constitution?

Some time – a fairly long while – afterwards, something similar happened to me when I was invoking the Name of Jesus Christ. I was obliged to stop pronouncing His Name: the effect was too much for me – my soul, wordlessly, without thought, trembled at the nearness of God. Then it was that the mystery of the priestly office was revealed to me.

The following day I celebrated the Liturgy, and Christ-God was in me, and with me, and outside me, and in the holy sacraments of His Body and Blood. And the Divine Name and the words of the liturgical texts issued from my mouth like a flame. I continued in this state for three days, after which the intensity of the experience diminished. But the Lord etched the memory of it on my mind and heart with a sharp tool. And I pray Him, 'Cast me not off in the time of old age; forsake me not when my strength faileth.'^{xxxviii.}

St. Paul bade us 'walk worthy of the vocation wherewith ye are called.'^{xxxix.} But what does this vocation consist of? Let us listen to him again: 'Unto me, who am less than the least of all saints, is this grace given that I should preach . . . the unsearchable riches of Christ; And to make all men see what

---

^{xxxvii.} Acts ii:3.
^{xxxviii.} Ps. lxxi:9.
^{xxxix.} Eph. iv:1.

47

is the fellowship of the mystery, which from the beginning of the world hath been hid in God, who created all things by Jesus Christ . . . In whom we have boldness and access with confidence by the faith of Him . . . that ye, being rooted and grounded in love, May be able to comprehend . . . what is the breadth, and length, and depth, and height; And to know the love of Christ . . . that ye might be filled with all the fulness of God. Now unto him that is able to do exceeding abundantly above all that we ask or think . . . be glory . . . throughout all ages, world without end.'[xl.]

So then our calling and mission is to become sons of our God and Father, through His only-begotten Son, of one substance with Him, everlasting and without beginning, and bearers of the *whole of divine plenitude*.[xli.]

Let me continue to tell of other happenings which could not be expected, seeing the sort of person I am. More than once it was given to me to contemplate Divine Light. In its tender embrace I would be filled with a love that is not of this earth. Sometimes the outside world lost its materiality and became invisible. What was happening to me belonged to another plane of being. And when in some unfathomable way everyday consciousness returned, a gentle sadness would pervade my soul.

Sometimes it would occur to me that it might have been possible for me not to 'return' – prayer, from being a temporary, could become an eternal state of the soul. The vision of Light is unfailingly accompanied by the grace that resurrects, and to abandon the earth when one is in that condition would be a blessing. We know that St. Seraphim of Sarov passed away while he was praying: his soul left his body before the body was dead – he was holding a lighted candle in his hand. 'Precious in the sight of the Lord is the death of his saints.'[xlii.] Should we not all depart thus from this life?

[xl.] cf. Eph. ch. iii.
[xli.] cf. John xvi: 27; xvii: 21–26.
[xlii.] Ps. cxvi: 15.

'Verily, verily, I say unto you, He that heareth my word, and believeth on him that sent me, *hath* everlasting life; and *shall not come* into condemnation; but is passed from death unto life.'[xliii] 'Verily, verily, I say unto you, If a man keep my saying, he shall never see death.'[xliv]

Prayer is energy of an especial order. It is the fusing of two actions – ours, the creature's, and that of the uncreated Divine. As such, it is both in the body and outside the body; even outside this world of space and time. When we are in blessed awe before the vision of God's holiness, and at the same time in despair at our extreme unworthiness of such a God, our prayer becomes a mighty uprush of the spirit that bursts through the tight ring of heavy matter. Our 'natural body must be raised a spiritual body,'[xlv] and become capable of following the spirit in its ultimate effort. The biological 'flesh and blood' body lacks the strength to emulate the spirit in its integral striving towards the Eternal God.[xlvi] 'Our conversation is in heaven; from whence also we look for the Saviour, the Lord Jesus Christ; Who shall change our vile body, that it may be fashioned like unto His glorious body, according to the working whereby he is able even to subdue all things unto himself.'[xlvii] 'If we then be spiritually risen with Christ, we naturally seek those things which are above in heaven, where Christ sitteth on the right hand of God.'[xlviii]

Oh, this gift of prayer! In its reaching-up to the beloved God the Father prayer is insatiable. Through prayer we enter into another form of being, not spatially but qualitatively surpassing this world. The soul, neither intoxicated by the imagination nor incited by rational philosophy, seeks paths where there are no paths. A certain intrinsic intuition prompts the soul which is held fast by the invisible but not

[xliii] John v: 24.
[xliv] John viii: 51.
[xlv] cf. I Cor. xv: 44.
[xlvi] cf. I Cor. xv: 50.
[xlvii] Phil. iii: 20–21.
[xlviii] cf. Col. iii: 1.

unbreakable chains of the 'law of sin' — chains which can be fractured, not by us but only with the help of the Almighty God, our Saviour. What can the soul's struggle for freedom be likened to? There is an analogy with the body in unbearable pain that twists and turns, trying to shake off its hurting. So does the soul writhe in prayerful weeping to smother her pain by being joined with God.

The Lord feels for us and often responds swiftly. But the contrary does happen, when all our appeals remain, as it were, unheard. The soul hangs suspended in space over the abyss, and is terrified, for God seems completely unattainable: He is outside all that exists. The mind finds no words that could reach the faraway Throne. Mute, with a silent cry, the soul prays in the desert of the world. Still, in her depths hope lurks. The sense of being abandoned by God disappears, and the sun comes out again.

From my own experience I can testify that there are two types of despair: the one, purely negative, destroys man, first spiritually and then physically. The other is a blessed despair. It is about this second form that I never stop talking. Through despair of this kind I was reborn into Light. It is not at all easy for me to confess to the world the goodwill towards me of the Most-High. I could never understand why this should be so with the likes of me. To begin with, a Light invisible to me showed me, first, my inner hell, and then the whole created world in its transitory existence, ever subject to the process of dying. I carried this dreadful vision within me for a long, long time. I was crushed by the absurdity of this world where nothing is eternal, where everything is marked by decay. But, strange as it may seem, abundant new life began to throb within me. An unbroken stream of prayer flooded my heart, luring my mind, too, often with growing strength; now so powerfully that it swept my spirit into an infinite expanse unlike anything that we ordinarily know. At one and the same time I was both cast down into nothingness and accorded invaluable experience of an intensified vision of the world, even to contact with eternity.

It is torture to be continually aware of one's destitute state. One feels stricken to the bone. But, a strange thing . . . when my contrition slackened, I felt as if I were dying spiritually. I could not understand what was happening. Only much later did Blessed Staretz Silouan explain to me, 'Thus does the Lord school us, lest we lose humility.' After that, I, too, was partly able to comprehend the secret of His way. I also discovered a certain analogy with what I had experienced as a painter: for a brief moment there comes a feeling of triumph, of victory. I have grasped what I was seeking! Surely I am close now to expressing the beauty spread before my eyes. But the rapture would soon disappear and once more I would be tormented by my failure. So it is – and even more so – with God: He does not leave us in peace. For a brief instant He comforts the soul, touches the heart with His fire, delights the mind with a vision of his glory . . . and again withdraws, lest we should think that we have attained to the fulness of knowledge of Him. Our lot on earth is to be 'poor in spirit'. The moment we are invaded by a false feeling of self-satisfaction, the Spirit of Life, proceeding from the Father forsakes us.

These fluctuating states made the pattern of the commandments of blessedness clear even to me – the foundation of all spiritual progress is an exhausting sense of our 'poverty'. But this acknowledgment is the source of energy for prayer, and at the same time a solid foundation on which to build the whole edifice of salvation until we arrive finally at our 'great reward in heaven.'[xlix.]

Again and again I would stress that pride is the root of all evil. In pride lie death and darkness. But holy *apatheia* (mastery over the passions) means humility which makes one feel that one is the lowest of all men, and in inexplicable fashion thereby raises one higher than all created beings.

[xlix.] cf. Matt. v: 3–16.

The Christian ascetic in his life in God is not to be likened to poet or writer, psychologist, philosopher or scholar. In his turning to God he looks forward instead of staying concentrated on himself. What he effectively experiences in prayer leaves an indelible mark on his being, which he will note in himself only much later, when he reflects on the past. The urge towards God at the outset is so intense that the spirit in its straining towards the Most-High contemplates Him alone. The soul of the repentant sinner, seeing himself inexpressibly far from the Truth that he seeks, becomes an aching wound and he beseeches the beloved Lord for mercy. The feeling of sin that destroys our being which was created in the likeness of God begets an indescribable regret for the state in which we have continued for so long; which had made us wholly unworthy of the Holy of holies. Could such a Lord accept me, utterly corrupt as I am? The soul stands, as it were, before the Last Judgment. And the more shattering her fear of sentence, the more urgent her prayer of repentance. It is impossible to say how long such prayer continues. When daily tasks interrupt one's physical standing before God, the essential attitude of the spirit does not alter but persists, turned Godward with all its powers.

In the fifth year of my monastic life the Abbot of the Monastery of St. Panteleimon, Archimandrite Missail, summoned me and put me 'under obedience' to learn Greek. The Monastery needed monks who knew the language used locally and therefore essential for all contacts, both spiritual and official, with the outside world. I made the traditional bow to receive blessing on the task before me. And when I was almost at the door he stopped me and said, 'Father Sophrony, God does not judge twice. If you carry out the task of obedience that I have laid upon you, *I* shall be responsible before God, you can abide in peace.' He said this with his head bowed on his chest as is usual in prayer. His voice was grave. Going straight to the library, I took out the books that I should need to study Greek, and returned to my cell. Opening the Attic Grammar, I concentrated on reading. And what happened? I had a physical sensation of my mind leaving my heart, rising to my forehead, and then moving in the direction of the book. At that moment I realised that for seven years my mind had stayed in my heart, engaged in repentant prayer. Remembering what the Abbot had said, I remained inwardly calm. Stricken with malaria, I struggled against my physical weakness in order to study for as many hours as possible every day. I remember once, while I was writing out an exercise and feeling exhausted, the thought occurring to me, If I were at this moment to hear the call to Judgment, how would it be with me? In the depths of my heart I felt tranquil. I would arise and go in peace to the Divine Judgment-Seat. I recall this particularly, because it was absolutely unlike my normal attitude of fear at the idea of judgment. Thus the Abbot's prayer gave me this experience of peace. My new occupation deprived me of the possibility of praying as I had previously, but grace in the most wonderful form of a hitherto-unknown peace never left me during the months of my efforts to learn Greek. Thus God did not abandon me, but neither did my heart withdraw from Him.

The months of study were over and the Lord vouchsafed that I should give myself again to desperate prayer of repentance. In order to be re-born in God it is necessary for us to feel appalled at ourselves as we are – to loathe the odious, ungodly passion of pride in us that drove us in disgrace from the Kingdom of the Father of lights. Salvation lies in Christ's commandment to love God and hate one's own life.[1] This is an extremely important subject, and I know that, however much I write, I cannot explore to the limit this side of the spiritual life of the Christian.

I have termed the despair that took possession of me a great gift from on High. But it was only after thirty years of struggle – perhaps longer – that I realised this. I did not seek outside help because I was caught up like a dry leaf in

[1] cf. Luke xiv: 26.

the wind which whirled me about, preventing me from understanding what was happening to me. I did not fathom the first thing. I could not ask anyone since I could not even formulate the question. Cosmic being stormily revealed itself to my mind with a rapidity that allowed my reason no time to linger on anything. It was like a madness but madness of a particular order, outside the competence of psychiatrists. The process began of leaving the world. Some obstacle lay between me and other people. I lost interest in being with them. One after another points of contact disappeared. The world of the arts – painting, music, poetry, literature, the theatre and so on – all that had formerly been the main content and meaning of my existence, paled and began to seem of no importance, often just childish amusement. And this was not easy for me: at times, in the first stage, I was torn between two centres of gravity, my painting and prayer, until prayer vanquished all other concerns of this world. There is only one objective – to find the true God, that is, the Creator of all being, and to live for ever in Him.

Is not such presumption lunacy on the part of a poor creature like myself? With God things are not at all easy or simple: He is too great for us. He is 'consuming fire'. He is Light inaccessible. He cast His fire on to our earth, and scorches our hearts. Yet even I am the work of His hands. He was clothed in our flesh that through this spectrum we might look on Him. Hence the hope that banishes all pessimism. 'Be of good cheer,' He said.[li] I believe that the appearance of this fire signals the Divine breath of eternity in us. Moreover, 'with God nothing shall be impossible . . . and blessed is she that believed: for there shall be a performance of those things which were told her from the Lord.'[lii]

Convinced by my own case of the instability of human nature, I live in a constant state of fear. It is known as fear of God and is not animal fear. It contains wisdom and

[li] John xvi: 33.
[lii] Luke i: 37, 45.

knowledge, love and power. But our encounter with the All-High God Whom we have not the strength to contain in ourselves, and Whom we cannot not love, makes us realise that we are still indescribably far from what should be the sacred purpose and point of our whole existence.

St. Peter on the Mount of Olives after the Last Supper rather emotionally declared, 'Though all men shall be offended because of thee, yet will I never be offended.' We all know what happened very soon after this confession of faith. 'And Peter remembered the word of Jesus, which said unto him, Before the cock crow, thou shalt deny me thrice. And he went out, and wept *bitterly*.'[liii.]

It is written, 'Perfect love casteth out fear . . . He that feareth is not made perfect in love.'[liv.] I know that I am not made perfect in love but this does not negate the fact that I do love God. And it is this very love that begets the fear in me of being unworthy of a response from God. I am stricken to the bone when I notice in myself even the slightest faltering. I do not remember any suspicion of doubt in my mind or heart during my years on Mt. Athos. But when I returned to Europe and came in contact with people who thought differently, I met with a latent energy in them which blew on my heart like a cold wind and perplexed my mind. Alien to the spirit of Christ, it disturbs one's inner peace for a while, and provokes the mind to a kind of conflict. What I had received by a gift from on High in my prayer of love in the desert eventually overcame the negative influences that I encountered: 'the law of the Spirit of life in Christ Jesus hath made me [also] free from' the power of this world.[lv.]

Peter recovered; but can I be sure for myself? So long as the heart is conscious of the presence of God, we are at peace and in a transport of love for Him. But when He withdraws and I no longer sense Him at work in me, my

[liii.] Matt. xxvi: 33, 75.
[liv.] I John iv: 18.
[lv.] cf. Rom. viii: 2.

infirmity again pains and distresses me. To one extent or another the way of the cross still continues to be mine in my old age. It seems to me that I now know the measure of man; and so no encounter can affect my freedom. But in the past I met with forces far too powerful for my mediocrity. In those terrible times the Name of Christ Jesus was my salvation. I pray that it will be thus with me even to the end, and without end. When God in His providence for us withdraws, the feeling of being forsaken kindles ardent prayer and in its embrace the soul joyously recognises her kinship with Christ, and likeness to Him grows. The *Lord* made us in His image. Therefore in Him we, too, become '*lords*'. Confirmed by His strength, we can behold all kinds of evil in the created world but the evil loses its power over us. Herein lies our 'lordship' which is indispensable for the 'kingdom which cannot be moved'.

'Yet once more I shake not the earth only, but also heaven. And this word, Yet once more, signifieth the removing of those things that are shaken, as of things that are made, that those things which cannot be shaken may remain.'[lvi.] We cannot know to what final ordeal all creation will be subjected. We must continue in reverent fear until we have crossed every created threshold to be fulfilled with the immortal life that proceeds from God.

The Church teaches that Jesus Christ took upon Himself the sins of the whole world. And he who prays to Him 'face to Face' in spirit assumes from Him the 'mind and feeling' that is in Him. And not the mind and feeling only, but prayer, too, like His prayer in Gethsemane. This is what we call 'hypostatic prayer'.

Whoever prays after this fashion enters into the plane of Divine life. And this is so even before his prayer has attained its full strength – the depth when prayer is accompanied by the tears one weeps for oneself, and maybe even more bitter tears. Thus said, thus wrote Staretz Silouan – that in praying

[lvi.] Heb. xii: 26–27.

for those who had cut themselves off from God he wept more than for himself.

Christ-God is infinite in His might: His Spirit fills every depth. But in His 'self-emptying' also, He is likewise unattainable for us. When we stand silently before God, the whole of our being laid bare, the profundities of our nature are unmasked for us, too. Total concentration – the pulling together of all that is within us, that makes our personality – shows us that the being of all mankind in its source and by its nature, is *one being, one man*. Hence the 'natural' impulse of our spirit to pray for all peoples, for *all Adam*, as for oneself. So do we interpret Christ's words, 'That they [all] may be one, even as we are one.'[lvii]

In repentant prayer for our sins we learn to experience the tragedy of all mankind through ourselves. If I suffer thus with my whole being because of my frustration at every turn; if my every fall mirrors the primordial Fall of our forefather Adam which wrenched all mankind from God our Father, it is natural that my personal sufferings should acquaint me existentially with the sufferings of all mankind. But the converse is also possible – in my joy I may behold the joy of the whole world. Thus he who has found the true way to his salvation in God learns to suffer with those that suffer, to rejoice with all who rejoice.

If sin in its profound essence is always a transgression against the Father's love, the love that has been destroyed can only be fully restored through total repentance, which should disclose to us – completely, if possible – what this crime signifies when we consider it on the plane of eternity.

O Father of all good, heal me, a leper.
Restore me who am corrupted by sin.
O Holy Father, hallow me – my mind, my heart, my very body.

[lvii] cf. John xvii: 21–23.

57

I have sinned before Thee, and now I die away from Thee.

Take me to Thee according to the abundance of Thy compassion and Thy mercy.

I would pray without forming any mental or visual images. My soul would detach herself from all that was transient, to concentrate with full strength on my God only. In an unaccountable way this total absence of visual forms or abstract concepts – as if everything in me halted though the life-force glowed richly – on my return to my usual state of perception gradually converted into *knowledge of being*.

The vision itself is unextended and spaceless: all condenses within into a minute prick. But attempt to put into words the knowledge perceived in those moments, and one is faced with a vast expanse of sea. I will try to set down briefly some of the thoughts that have occurred to me.

Every creature having reason swings between two extremes – between love for God to the point of self-hatred, and love of self to the point of hatred for God. 'Hate' for God means a falling away, a withdrawal from God. It is not necessarily linked with emotions of the heart, though this, too, may often happen. Hate can be a cool decision on the part of the intellect – the 'enlightened' intellect, many would say, but reality is hid from them: their 'light' may naturally evolve to a degree where all life is frozen out.

There are innumerable intermediate states. In the middle we find the great mass of inert souls having no clear awareness of their existence or any definitely chosen direction. But the nearer we approach the frontiers, the more dynamic becomes the impetus of the spirit, the more compelled we feel to make a final *choice*. Each will select what he has loved more.

To approach in spirit the last boundaries, as it were, still does not mean crossing the threshold of the temporal, to enter the realm of eternal being. Both age-old ascetic experience and revelation declare that the created spirit can spurn the objective that he has actually reached and like lightning[lviii.] flash across the abyss to settle on the opposite shore.

Both separate individuals and great multitudes can renounce the One True Being – the 'I AM THAT I AM'.

God had set no limits for any of us on the spiritual plane. '*All things* are lawful . . .' but we must not be 'brought under the power of any.'[lix.] If man were not endowed with this freedom his divinisation would be out of the question. Created in the image of the All–High, man cannot be subject to constraint of any sort where ultimate spiritual self–determination in eternity is concerned. God reveals Himself to us as 'Light in which there is no darkness at all.'[lx.] He showed Himself as having loved us 'unto the end.'[lxi.] But He does not impose Himself on us by force: it depends on us whether to accept or reject His gift of love – and this not only while we are in this life but, more especially, in eternity also.

We are called to eternal life in the Kingdom of our Father Which is in heaven. But entry into the Kingdom for created beings inevitably entails great suffering. Many decline the Father's gift of love precisely because the utmost effort is required to assimilate it. How many times did I say to myself at first, 'Oh no . . . if that is the cost; I don't want even this gift.' But strong are 'the hands of the living God,' and 'it is a fearful thing to fall into them.'[lxii.]

He had set His seal on my heart, and love for Him was stronger than death. I had only to think for an instant of departing from Him, to find myself plunged in murky darkness.[lxiii.] I saw that to withdraw from Him would be death. Life lay forward only, in a hand–to–hand struggle. Staretz Silouan explained to me how those afflicted with pride faced a hard fight. The painfulness of the effort, however, showed

[lviii.] cf. Luke x: 18; xxiii: 42–43.
[lix.] cf. I Cor. vi: 12.
[lx.] cf. I John i: 5.
[lxi.] cf. John xiii: 1.
[lxii.] cf. Heb. x: 31.
[lxiii.] cf. John vi: 68.

59

me that if I willingly accepted the battle, it meant that I was free. The very suffering involved was reliable proof of our freedom as reasonable beings. It became quite clear to me that the Kingdom is only to be taken 'by force;'[lxiv.] that I, too, must travel the way that likens man to Christ, Who is 'the way.'[lxv.]

[lxiv.] Matt. xi: 12.
[lxv.] John xiv: 6.

III

Again, On PRAYER

Nowadays there are people all over the world in search of a solution to their quest. This widespread unallayed spiritual thirst is a historical event that is really tragic. Many are on the edge of despair. Every one of them, according to his own measure, in the depths of his spirit suffers from the absurdity of contemporary life. They are inconsolable in their grief; their own individual efforts are not enough to free them from the enclosing world of confusion, and stay their minds on the most important thing of all.[i]

Ours is sometimes called the post-Christian age. But I personally, from what I know of the history of the world and of Christianity, am convinced that Christianity in its true dimensions has never yet been properly grasped by the great mass of people. Kingdoms pretending to the name of 'Christian', and their peoples, have worn the mask of piety, while 'denying the power thereof.'[ii] They have lived, and live, like heathens. Strange as it may be, it is precisely the Christian countries who keep the greater part of the universe in the iron grip of slavery. In these latter years they have shrouded the world in a dark cloud of expectation of apocalyptic fire: 'the heavens and the earth, which are now . . . reserved unto fire against the day of judgment and perdition of ungodly men.'[iii]

In the present crisis of Christianity among the popular

[i] cf. Luke x: 42.
[ii] cf. II Tim. iii: 5.
[iii] II Pet. iii: 7; Luke xxi: 34–35.

61

masses it is quite justifiable to discern a rebellion of the natural conscience against the distortions which the Gospel teaching has suffered in its historical destinies.

We are living again in the atmosphere of the first centuries of our era: unto us 'it is given in the behalf of Christ, not only to believe on him, but also to suffer for his sake'.[iv] More than once have I rejoiced in the thought that, for the most part, my life has coincided with harassment of Christianity. This allows me the more acutely to feel myself a Christian, to realise the incomparable honour in times like these of following the only-begotten Son of the Father on His path to Golgotha. Persecution is rife everywhere but in different forms – none of which, however, is easy to bear. May the God of love deliver every soul from the calamity of being a tormentor even of 'one of these little ones.'[v]

In 'suffering for his sake'[vi] there is an especial blessing and even election: he who suffers, by the very force of circumstances places himself in constant association with Jesus Christ, is led into the sphere of Divine love and becomes God-bearing.

There are two ways for theology: the one, widely familiar in previous centuries, appertaining to the professional theologian; the other, which means being crucified with Christ,[vii] knowing Him in the secret places of the heart. The first of these types is accessible to the majority of the intellectually endowed having a preference for philosophical subjects – genuine belief in the Divinity of Christ expressing itself in a life lived according to the spirit of His commandments is not needed. The second is the theology of the confessors, which is born of a profound fear of God in the fiery flames of repentance, leading to existential reality through the

[iv] Phil. i: 29.
[v] Matt. xviii: 10.
[vi] cf. Phil. i: 29.
[vii] cf. I Pet. 4: 13; Rom. 8: 17; II Tim. 2: 11–12; Phil. 3:10; Rev. 1:9 *et al.*

appearance of Uncreated Light. Academic theology combined with living faith affords blessed results. But it can easily degenerate into abstract theory, and cease to be what we see in the lives of the Apostles, Prophets, Fathers – the direct action of God in us. 'No man can come to me, except the Father which hath sent me draw him . . . It is written in the prophets, And they shall be all taught of God. Every man therefore that hath heard' [in his heart] 'and hath learned of the Father, cometh unto me.'[viii.]

The Holy Trinity is the God of Love. The love of which the Gospel treats is the uncreated life-force of unoriginate Divinity. The property of this Love is to unite us in very being. He who dwells in this unity with God gradually grows to realise what is happening to him. 'But God hath revealed [knowledge of Him] unto us by his Spirit: for the Spirit searcheth all things, yea, the deep things of God . . . We have received, not the spirit of the world, but the spirit which is of God: that we might know the things that are freely given to us of God. Which things also we speak, not in the words which man's wisdom teacheth, but which the Holy Ghost teacheth'.[ix.] 'Thou art the Christ, the Son of the living God.'[x.] And as Jesus answered, 'flesh and blood hath not revealed unto him [Peter], but my Father which is in heaven.'[xi.] 'Great is the mystery of godliness: God was manifest in the flesh, justified in the Spirit, seen of angels, preached unto the Gentiles, believed on in the world, received up into glory.'[xii.] And this is natural growth in the Spirit through dwelling in the Divine realm by keeping Christ's commandments. The mind straightway apprehends knowledge and formulates it in human terms. It happens like a flash of lightning, when the heart is burning with love. This is the 'marvellous light'

[viii.] John vi: 44–45.
[ix.] cf. I Cor. II: 10–13.
[x.] Matt. xvi: 16.
[xi.] cf. Matt. xvi: 17.
[xii.] I Tim. iii: 16.

of eternity to which we are called.[xiii.] The accumulation in the experience of the Church of such 'moments' of enlightenment has led organically to their reduction into one whole. This is how the first attempt at the systemization of a live theology came about, the work of St. John of Damascus, a man rich, too, in personal experience. The disruption of this wondrous ascent to God in the unfathomable wealth of higher intellection is brought about, where there is a decline of personal experience, by a tendency to submit the gifts of Revelation to the critical faculty of our reason – by a leaning towards 'philosophy of religion'. The consequences are scholastic accounts of theology in which, again, there is more philosophy than Spirit of life.

The substance of the life of the one who prays intensely resembles a boundless ocean of living waters. The spirit is continually enriched but not so much by the large number of new words or conceptions as by the intensification of experiences already acquired and familiar. In preceding pages I have tried to present instances of the subtle and at the same time deep-rooted ascetic struggle against the passions that destroy us. For years – tens of years, even – numerous alternations of suffering with consolation from above train our spirit, making it more capable of new forms of thinking and of acceptance of being in general. The mind accustoms itself sightlessly to contemplate the whole world, while the spirit, prayerfully, in tender pain, bears in itself this world and its associations. Such an act of spiritual synthesis contains the mature prayer of the Christian standing before God with all his mind, with all his heart in their fusion together. Incapable of expressing in words all that he bears within himself, the ascetic striver not seldom prays wordlessly – but again, in global grasp of all that he has perceived, or in total absorption in God to the point of oblivion of the earth. In this seemingly-loose description of the processes of the life of the

[xiii.] cf. I Pet. ii: 9.

spirit we are talking of the gradual transition from individual forms of being into the hypostatic-personal form of being in the eternal God. To give a systematized, analytical outline of this ascent into life is impossible. We do not find it even in the works of the great Fathers of our Church. A scholastic systematization of material is possible to a certain extent in conceptual theological works but never, in no way, in living words concerning the genuine life of our spirit.

Effectively to be in God and with God is given either to 'little children'[xiv] or to 'fools for Christ's sake,'[xv] like the great Apostle Paul. He wrote of himself: 'But what things were gain to me, those I counted loss for Christ. Yea doubtless, and I count all things but loss for the excellency of the knowledge of Christ Jesus my Lord: for whom I have suffered the loss of all things, and do count them but dung, that I may win Christ . . . That I may know him, and the power of his resurrection, and the fellowship of his sufferings, being made conformable unto his death; If by any means I might attain unto the resurrection of the dead.'[xvi] Paul obeyed the Lord's commandment: 'So likewise, whosoever he be of you that forsaketh not all that he hath, he cannot be my disciple'[xvii] – 'all that he hath' on the plane of created being, when separated from God, in its self-affirmation. 'They which are of faith, the same are the children of Abraham . . . and are blessed with him.'[xviii] Thus, we must follow the example of our spiritual ancestor Abraham – take the fire in our hand, and the knife, and go up into a high place, to bring to God the burnt offering of all that we hold dear in the flesh. Then we, too, shall hear, 'Now I know thee . . . and in blessing I will bless thee.'[xix] And this is the true path to a blessed

[xiv] cf. Matt. xviii: 3; xi: 25.
[xv] cf. I Cor. iv: 8–10; i: 20.
[xvi] cf. Phil. iii: 7–11.
[xvii] Luke xiv: 33.
[xviii] cf. Gal. iii: 7–9 and 29.
[xix] cf. Gen. chap. xxii.

eternity: every other path holds the traces of death. Only devoted following of Christ 'unto the end'[xx] can reveal the higher potentials of our nature and make us capable of apprehending the Gospel in its eternal dimension. The resolution to 'forsake all'[xxi] brings us to the threshold between time and eternity, and we begin to contemplate the reality of another, imperishable Being, hitherto concealed from us. God does not violate our freedom. He will not force Himself into our heart if we are not disposed to open the door to Him. 'Behold, I stand at the door, and knock: if any man hear my voice, and open the door, I will come in to him.'[xxii] And the wider we open our hearts, the more abundantly does the Uncreated Light flood into our inner world.

The love we feel for God, together with the experience of His love for us, radically alters both our state of mind and our thinking. Hostility of any kind between people – brethren – seems like appalling folly. We all of us have a single enemy – our mortality. If man is mortal, if there is no resurrection, then the whole of world history is nothing but senseless creature suffering. Even love here below is interwoven with death: to love means dying. And our spirit longs to cross into the light-bearing sphere where there is no obstacle to insatiable love; where the insatiable desire is none other than the supreme dynamic of life, of the 'more abundant life' that Christ gives.[xxiii]

The approach to sublime prayer is closely linked with deep repentance for our sins. When the bitter taste of this cup becomes unbearable, timeless pain and self-disgust are suddenly and unexpectedly transformed by the touch of God's love. Suddenly, everything is different, and we are oblivious

[xx] John xiii: 1.
[xxi] cf. Matt. xix: 27–30.
[xxii] Rev. iii: 20.
[xxiii] cf. John x: 10.

to the world. Many give the label *ecstasy* (*rapture*) to this kind of phenomenon. I do not care for the word – various distortions are associated with it. But if we changed the name of this Divine gift, called it the penitent soul's immersion in God, then, too, I must say that it has never occurred to me to cultivate – that is, seek artificial means to arrive at – such a state. But it would come, unforeseen, and in a different fashion every time. The only thing that I remember – and this I know for a fact – is my inconsolable distress at the remoteness of God which had somehow become linked with my soul. I repented of my fallen state acutely. And had I had the physical strength, there would have been no end to my lamentation.

There, I have written it down and not without sadness I remember the days – or, rather, nights – of yore when my mind and heart so positively forsook my old life that for years I never looked back on the past. I would even forget my spiritual stumblings but the shattering vision of my unworthiness of this Holy God grew ever more intense.

On more than one occasion I felt as if I were crucified on an invisible cross. This would happen on Mt. Athos when I got angry with those who vexed me. My wickedness would destroy prayer and fill me with horror. At times it seemed impossible to struggle against it – it lacerated me like a wild beast tearing its prey to pieces. Once because of a flash of irritation prayer departed from me. I had to struggle for eight months in order to find it again. But when the Lord yielded to my tears, my heart took courage and I became more patient.

This experience of crucifixion happened again later (when I was back in France) but in a different form. I would never refuse to accept the task of caring, as a spiritual father, for those who turned to me for help. My heart felt especial compassion for the mentally ill. Overwhelmed by the monstrous difficulties of contemporary life, some of them would try to insist on prolonged attention that I had not the strength for. My position became desperate: whichever way I turned, someone would be crying out in pain. This revealed to me the depths of suffering in our times, with people shattered by the cruelty of our famous civilisation. Colossal state mechanisms, although set up by men, are impersonal, not to say inhuman apparatus, indifferently crushing millions of lives. Powerless as I was to change the actually intolerable though legitimized crimes of society, in my prayer, away from any visible images, I felt the presence of the crucified Christ. I lived His suffering in spirit so distinctly that a physical vision of His being 'lifted up from the earth'[xxiv.] could in no way have intensified my participation in His pain. However insignificant my experiences may have been, they deepened my perception of Christ in His earthly coming to save the world.

A wondrous revelation is given to us in Him. He attracts our spirit to Himself by the magnitude of His love. Weeping, my soul blessed, and blesses, our God and Father, Who deigns to reveal to us through the Holy Spirit the incomparable holiness and truth of His Son, by means of the small trials we are put to.

The measure of grace conferred at the beginning to attract and instruct may be no less than that accorded to the perfect. However, this does not at all mean that the fearful blessing is assimilated by those who have received it. The adoption of God's gift requires long probation and hard striving. Altogether, there are three stages to the rebirth of fallen man and the putting on of the new.[xxv.] The first, the initial stage, is the summons and the inspiration to embark on the ascetic struggle; the second happens when the feeling of grace is replaced by a sense of being abandoned by God, the point of which is to afford the ascetic striver the possibility of *volunteering* fidelity to God. The third and final stage is the acquisition, for the second time, and preservation of 'perceptible' grace, linked now with intelligent cognition of God.

[xxiv.] John xii: 32.
[xxv.] cf. Eph. iv: 22–24.

'He that is faithful in that which is least is faithful also in much . . . If therefore ye have not been faithful in the unrighteous mammon, who will commit to your trust the true riches? And if ye have not been faithful in that which is another man's, who shall give you that which is your own?'[xxvi.] He who in the initial period has been directed by the very action of grace to prayer and every other good work, and through a prolonged time of being forsaken by God goes on living as if grace continued immutable with him, will, after long testing of his faithfulness, receive the 'true' riches, to possess imprescriptibly for ever. In other words, grace and created nature knit together and become one. This final gift is the divinisation of man; the communication to him of the divine form of being, without beginning, hallowed. It is the transfiguration of the whole man through which he becomes Christ-like, perfect.

Those who 'have not been faithful in that which is another man's', as Christ expressed it, will lose what they received at the outset. Here we can detect a certain parallel with the parable of the talents: '. . . he delivered unto them his goods. And unto one he gave five talents, to another two, and to another one; to every man according to his several ability . . . And after a *long* time the lord of those servants cometh, and reckoneth with them. And so he that had received five talents, . . . brought other five talents, saying, Lord, thou deliveredst unto me five talents: behold, I have gained beside them five talents more. His lord said unto him, Well done, thou good and faithful servant: thou hast been faithful over a few things, I will make thee ruler over many things: *enter thou into the joy of thy lord.* He also that had received two talents came and said, Lord, thou deliveredst unto me two talents: behold, I have gained two other talents beside them . . . Well done, good and faithful servant; thou hast been faithful over a few things, I will make thee ruler over

[xxvi.] Luke xvi: 10–12.

many things: *enter thou into the joy of thy lord.* Then he which had received the one talent came and said, Lord, I knew thee that thou art an hard man ... And I was afraid, and went and hid thy talent in the earth: lo, there thou hast that is thine. His lord answered and said unto him, Thou wicked and slothful servant ... Take therefore the talent from him, and give it unto *him which hath* ten talents ... but from him that hath not shall be taken away even that which he hath.'[xxvii.]

And this parable, like the preceding one, does not apply to ordinary human relations but only to God: the Lord did not take away from the servant who had laboured and doubled his talents but gave him all — the original talents and those he had gained by his labour — to possess as co-owner. '*Enter thou into the joy* [of the possession of the kingdom] *of thy lord.*' And when the talent that had not been made use of is returned, the Lord gives that, too, 'unto him which hath ten' ... 'for unto every one' that labours over the Divine gifts, '*shall be given, and he shall have abundance.*'[xxviii.]

St. John Climacus (St. John of the Ladder) says that it is possible to familiarize oneself with every form of science, of art, and every profession, and practise it without any special effort. But no one has ever been able to pray without toil — particularly if it is a case of the concentrated prayer of the mind in the heart. Anyone feeling strongly drawn to this kind of prayer may find himself faced with a wish — difficult to realise — a desire to hide away, burrow into the depths of the earth, where even the light of the sun is not seen, where the sound of human pain, or human joy, is not heard, and every transitory care is left behind. This is understandable: it is normal to conceal one's intimate life from strangers, and prayer of this kind bares the very kernel of the soul,

[xxvii.] Matt. xxv: 14 *et seq.*
[xxviii.] Matt. xxv: 29.

which is unable to endure any contact save that of the hand of our Creator.

To what agonising tensions man is exposed in his attempts to find the right place for the prayer he seeks! Like a breath from another world this prayer attracts various conflicts, inner and outer. One of these is the struggle with one's own body which is not slow to disclose its impotence to keep up with the aspirations of the spirit – often physical needs reach such a pitch that the spirit is forced to come down from the heights of prayer to look after the body, lest it die.

Another point that has to be wrestled with, especially in the first stages – how is it possible to ignore our neighbour whom we are bidden to love as ourself? Theologically, detachment for the sake of prayer appears to be contrary to the purport of the commandment; ethically, it seems like inadmissible 'egoism'; mystically, like sinking into the darkness of divestment, where there is no support for the spirit, where one loses consciousness of the reality of the world. And, finally, there is fear, because we do not know whether our undertaking is pleasing to the Lord.

The ascetic divestment of all that is created when merely consequent on an effort of our human will is too negative. The mind sees that a negative act, as such, cannot lead to positive, concrete possession of what we seek. But it is impossible to expound all the hesitations of the mind at such times. One of them – I have renounced all that is ephemeral but God is not with me. Is not this 'outer darkness' – hell itself? The seeker after pure prayer will find himself in many another equally wretched state. It may be that this is inevitable. Experience shows that it is normal for prayer to penetrate the vast realm of cosmic being.

By their very nature Christ's commandments surmount all restrictions. The soul stands over abysses where our unenlightened spirit sees no way. What shall I do? I cannot manage the yawning abyss. I see how small and impotent I am. I stumble and fall. But my soul has committed herself into the hands of the Living God, and I instinctively turn to Him, and without difficulty He reaches me wherever I am.

At first the soul is alarmed but having many a time been saved by prayer, is gradually fortified in hope and becomes more valiant where formerly courage seemed misplaced.

I am trying to write about the unseen battle of our spirit. The experiences that I have known have not given sufficient grounds for accounting them as eternity acquired here and now. I think that so long as we are in this material body we cannot help making analogies pertaining to the visible world. How it will be when we finally step across from the physical and the temporal is still unknown. I repeat – in that expanse there are no visible paths. Fear – not animal fear – strains our attention to the utmost. Only prayer can hold us steady when everything else swings to and fro. The soul silently laments, or utters a brief cry, 'Lord, save me.'[xxix.]

I remember the time when I gave up painting and, so it seemed, committed myself wholly to Christ. A great many eminent representatives of Russian culture – spiritual and humanist – were then saying, not indifferently, that the world had entered a tragic epoch: that everyone who lived responsibly had to realise the moral necessity of sharing in the tragedy that gripped the whole universe, joining in, participating, so far as possible, in the search for a happy issue; and so on, and so on. I would listen to these remarkable people with profound respect but could not follow in their steps: an inner voice told me that such a part was not for me. And so I continued to beseech God to bring me to the place, the environment, where I, poor ignoramus, might find salvation. In my prayers I propounded my plan to God, my time-table; and He performed it all with mathematical precision. I was cast by a loving hand into the ascetic *milieu* of Mt. Athos.

There, on the Holy Mountain, I found the circumstances I needed – long church services, for the most part at night; simple tasks that demanded no intellectual exertion; the

[xxix.] Matt. xiv: 30.

opportunity to live under obedience without having to think how the abbot and his associates, the monastery elders, regulated the cloister. Free from all worldly cares, I could pray without interruption, day and night. Little time was left for reading, half an hour or less in the twenty-four hours. But the Lord was with me; and I could not tear myself away from Him even for a moment. My heart burned constantly. My mind clung to the rock-face, as it were, of God's word. Enemy forces could provoke no impulse alien to the Spirit of Christ in my soul. I prayed horror-stricken at what I had been, and still was. Heart and mind became the battle-ground for the fight between Christ and the Enemy, a colossus of cosmic dimensions. During that period I trod an invisible rope over bottomless pits. A curious despair would seize on me from all sides, like the sea embracing a drowning man. I say 'curious' because when the feeling of despair abated, I was somehow left dying spiritually. Like a volcano this despair provoked ardent prayer. Like St. Peter I cried to Christ, the Almighty, 'Lord, save me'.

Thus, in this uneven rhythm, the months and years went by. It is impossible to describe it all. Later on I came to realise that I was visited thus because of my proud, mad fall. I saw that following Christ-God casts man naturally, as it were, into the shoreless oceans of the spirit. To live in Christ means perceiving Him as the veritable Conqueror of death: 'I am come a light into the world . . . not to judge the world, but to save the world'[xxx] . . . 'My sheep . . . follow me: And I give unto them eternal life; and they shall never perish, neither shall any man pluck them out of my hand.'[xxxi]

In those days I seized upon the audacious words of St. Isaac of Syria:[xxxii] 'Do not liken those who work signs and wonders in the world to the anchoret having knowledge. Prefer the inaction of silence rather than the feeding of the

[xxx] John xii: 46–47.
[xxxi] John x: 27–28 *et al.*
[xxxii] Discourse 56.

hungry and the conversion of many peoples to the worship of God.' I have never ventured to compare myself with the Fathers or quite apply their sayings to my own case but a certain similarity of experience must be present, otherwise we should for ever be left without true knowledge of spiritual realities. My mind never took the risk of exploring sufficiently St. Isaac's state when he spoke of this vision that transcends the measure of man. And at this point I will say only a very little about myself.

God's goodness towards me, which I could not fully realise, in the first years of my turning to Christ cast me cruelly into a boundless world, making me aware of my nothingness, my wasted state. This gift from God cleansed my heart from the deadly ulcer of pride, and enabled me in love and peace to contemplate God – and receive new, imperishable life from Him.

Descendants of Adam, we all carry within us the consequences of his fall, of which the Scriptures speak, but we do not all discern to the same degree the ontological extent of this calamity. A profound psycho-analysis of man – the image of God – begins in the first pages of the Biblical Revelation, not in the lying-in hospital. Pride, as the manifest or hidden tendency to self-divinisation, has distorted the human heart: no sooner do we detect in ourselves some sign of spiritual ascension than this snake lifts its head and thereby clouds the mind, interrupts the vision, and drives us away from God. Now I see that my extreme ignorance at the outset saved me. In my desperate prayer of repentance the Lord gave me direct precepts, and vanity was stayed from me. One is forced to the conclusion that the utterly contrite spirit is capable of apprehending Divine action. The passage from St. Isaac quoted above corresponded to my own spiritual history in the sense that to know the true God took on more importance for me than any event in the political life of the world. My thirst for God was more vital than everything else on earth. Without this knowledge – of man and of God – I felt benighted; apart from Christ there was no exit from the dark cellar. Worse, in the whole universe I saw nothing but a hideous tangle of human passions – a Gordian knot that no sword could cut.

'A man is born into the world.'[xxxiii] I saw this through Christ. Man, godlike hypostasis, is born as potentiality; goes through the process of becoming, at first in the confines of this world, after which he must attain supra-cosmic dimensions by following Christ Who overcame the world (the cosmos): 'Be of good cheer; I have overcome the world.'[xxxiv]

I repeat: The Lord gave me the grace of being mindful of death, together with a blessed despair. 'Being mindful of death' places one face to face with eternity, to begin with in its negative aspect, when all existence is seen to be in the grip of death. Next, the Light of the Theophany of our Lord descends on the soul, bringing victory over death. The 'despair' came with my recognition of how far I was from God. These two – being mindful of death, and despair – were the wings that carried me across the abyss. This fearful and long-drawn-out experience was a blessing from God, thanks to which the 'vail was taken away from my heart' which prevented me from understanding the New Testament Revelation in Christ and in the Holy Spirit.[xxxv]

All that is preposterous and frightful in the outside world, everything that is banal and tedious in daily life, resolves into a contradictory yet grandiose *tableau*. Both the noble and the ignoble somehow or other find their reflection in each of us. The manifold contrasts – of evil and good, ignorance and light, grief and joy, folly and wisdom, love and hatred, weakness and strength, construction and destruction, birth and death – all go to form the all-embracing vision of Being. The innumerable multitude of vexations and insults imposed

[xxxiii] John xvi: 21.
[xxxiv] John xvi: 33.
[xxxv] cf. II Cor. iii: 13–18.

on us degrade and put us to scorn. The soul despairs before such a spectacle. And suddenly the meaning of Christ's words, 'A MAN IS BORN INTO THE WORLD' becomes clear in their eternal significance, eternal even for God. And for this joy all previous ills and sorrows are remembered no more.

Christ's commandents are expressed in a few simple words but in a miraculous fashion when we obey them our spirit unfolds in longing to embrace 'all things which are in heaven, and which are on earth'[xxxvi.] in the love commanded of us. Surely it is inconceivable that creatures brought into being from 'nothing' could be possessed of such power? Of course, it is impossible for us, of ourselves, to contain in our heart the whole universe. But the Maker of all that exists Himself appeared in our form of being and effectively demonstrated that our nature was conceived not only with the ability to embrace the created cosmos but also to assume the plenitude of Divine life. Without Him we can do nothing[xxxvii.] but with Him and in Him everything becomes attainable – though not without 'pain'. Pain is essential, firstly to make us realise that we are free *personae* (hypostases), and secondly that on the day of Judgment the Lord might give us His life for us to possess for ever.[xxxviii.]

To transport ourselves in mind, whenever we suffer tribulation, into universal dimensions makes us like unto Christ. If we do this, everything that happens to us individually will be a revelation of what happens in the wide world. Streams of cosmic life will flow through us, and we shall be able, through personal experience to discern both man in his temporal existence and even the Son of man in His two natures. It is precisely thus, through suffering, that we grow

[xxxvi.] cf. Eph. i: 10.
[xxxvii.] cf. John xv: 5.
[xxxviii.] cf. Luke xvi: 10–12.

to cosmic and meta-cosmic self-consciousness. By going through the trial of self-emptying in following Christ, crucifying ourselves with Him, we become receptive to the infinitely great Divine Being. In wearying penitential prayer for the whole world, we merge ourselves spiritually with all mankind: we become universal in the image of the universality of Christ Himself, Who bears in Himself all that exists. Dying with Him and in Him, we here and now anticipate resurrection.

The Lord suffered for every one of us. His sufferings do indeed cover all our ills since the fall of Adam. In order to know Christ properly, it is essential that we ourselves enter into His anguish, and experience it *all*, if this be possible, as He Himself did. Thus, and only thus, is Christ-God made known, existentially – i.e., not abstractly, through psychological or theoretical faith that is not converted into deeds.

From the outset when I returned to Christ, with a little more understanding now of Who Jesus was, my heart underwent a change and my thoughts took a different direction. From my inner conflicts I spontaneously shifted to humanity at large, and found myself suffering with all mankind. The experience made me see that we must not only live the ordeals that fall to our lot within the narrow framework of our individuality but must transfer them in spirit to the universal plane – in other words, realise that the same cosmic life that flows through us flows in the veins of everyone else. Because of this apparently natural psychological impulse, I began to feel all the ills – disease, disasters, feuds, enmities, natural catastrophes, wars, and so on – that befall the human race, with increased compassion. This really quite normal compulsion was to bring forth precious fruit for me: I learned to live the fate of all mankind as if it were happening to me personally. It is precisely this that is enjoined by the commandment, 'Thou shalt love thy neighbour as thyself'[xxxix]. – neighbour, of course, in the Christian interpretation of the word.[xl] Developing and growing stronger with the years, my cognition naturally extended to the ends of the earth, and beyond – to the Infinite. With gratitude to God I looked back on all the calamities of the First World War: the terrible disruption of the administrative life of the country; the revolutionary battle waged the length and breadth of Russia that endangered each and everyone; the acute shortages of everything necessary for normal living; the alienation from all that is important and dear to the soul and mind; the agonising idiocy of everything that was happening . . . That was how I conceived of the tragedy of contemporary history. Later I fathomed its sources – in the Biblical narrative of the Fall of man.

A terrible scene. And still not the end: 'Yet once more I shake not the earth only, but also heaven'.[xli]

Thus I draw nearer to the great mystery of the 'image of God' in us: the *Persona*. He revealed Himself to us in the Name – I AM THAT I AM. Yes, we are in His image. Standing before Him in prayer, our spirit at one and the same time both glories and bewails – glories in the contemplation of realities excelling earthly imagination; bewails its nothingness, its complete impotence to contain the Divine gift. Thus from the very outset of our birth from on High the soul pines. To be sure, we do grow but the process seems to us a slow and painful one. It can be said that the whole of Christian life consists of the 'pain of bringing forth' for eternity.[xlii]

I notice that my mind continually returns to one and the same vision, from which I cannot detach myself, to which I

[xxxix] Matt. xxii: 39.
[xl] cf. Luke x: 29–37.
[xli] Heb. xii: 26.
[xlii] cf. *Septuagint* Isaiah xxvi: 17–18.

began to relate over half a century ago. The Lord absorbs me completely. I both see and do not see my surroundings. My eye glances around at intervals when I am busy with the unavoidable preoccupations of everyday life. But whether I am asleep or awake, God is closer to me than the air I breathe. During the past decades grace in diverse forms has streamed down on me, sometimes like a wide river, sometimes like a cascade of 'living water'[xliii] on my head. On occasions – it still happens – a boundless expanse of ocean would open out before me; or like a weightless puppet I would hang suspended over a peculiar imaginary abyss . . . and here I lose myself: what I have written is but a rough impression in a painter's sketch-book of a majestic panorama. My soul would sing hymns of praise to God, Who with such love came to meet me, a thing of nought, but I cannot find words worthy of Him.

[xliii] John iv: 10.

IV

SPIRITUAL LIFE

Of my own will I plunged into the thick darkness. I wanted to cut myself off from life so 'full of the habitations of cruelty,'[i] and set out in search of immutable being. In my career as a painter there had been fleeting moments when it seemed to me that I beheld the miracle of beauty, and I would try to retain those moments. But nothing lasted. Corruption was universal.

What exactly was it that oppressed me? Repugnance against the absurdity of everything that was condemned to destruction. The idea of dissolution filled me with dread and disgust. Death is no solution to the problem – I saw death as the final negation of all that exists. 'The earth also and the works that are therein'[ii] seemed doomed. Salvation was nowhere to be found.

My longing for immutable, absolute being exhausted me. In the depths of my heart I believed that there was some other form of being uninfected with the poison of decay. I set out on an abortive path, hoping to free myself from the earthly manner of life by imbuing my mind with the idea of 'pure being'. Misconstruing the Gospel, I made an insane choice, the essence of which meant returning into the non-being from which the Creator had called all of us. It was a long time before I realised my error.

My spirit continued in a state of tension. The changes in my inner humour affected my thoughts – each new experi-

[i] Ps. lxxiv: 20.
[ii] cf. II Pet. iii: 10.

ence in one way or another upset some former conviction, thereby proving that the mind in its given frame is incapable of stablishing itself once and for all in the sought-for Truth.

And so I arrived at the frontier beyond which thought can proceed no further, and my whole being became one long expectation of the coming of the Spirit of Truth.

'I AM THAT I AM.' It is impossible to detect the actual process of our inner growth. I think this may be because our spirit thirsts for 'those things which cannot be shaken'[iii] – that are not subject to progression. A life of profound prayer is a combination of our natural upsurges towards the eternal Being and the eternal Being's descent to us. When the One true God reveals Himself to us we are introduced into the sphere of His Being and undergo a radical alteration in our whole self not to be defined in ordinary language. We are too circumscribed to contain the gift completely. Nevertheless, our heart experiences an indescribable harmony of love, and the mind falls silent, astounded by the inconceivable vision.

Over the years God's word would come into my heart and mind, and I noticed how in the briefest of utterances the Lord reveals infinitude at the point where our praying spirit happens to be concentrated. A brief sentence encompasses both the height of the vision and the depth of knowledge. Our spirit is led by some mysterious force and in some inscrutable fashion to the very reality of the Eternal God. Events like these do not depend on man but on God's good will towards His suffering creature. We cannot foresee when He will incline to us, and in what form. We only yearn for Him; weep in repentance over our perversion; long for Him to heal us; weary of being separated from Him.

Anyone to whom God unexpectedly shews mercy is disin-

[iii] Heb. xii: 27–28.

clined to talk about the gift from on High. On the contrary, he will 'keep all these things, and ponder them in his heart.'[iv] So it has been with me during the half-century or so of my ascetic striving. But now, having decided on this act of witness, I still cannot find either the words or the means to convey to others my experience, at times so compelling. In the convergence of directions – mine 'from beneath,' His 'from above'[v] – I suddenly discovered Him in me under the name 'I AM'. That was my turning-point: I perceived Being in a different perspective, the opposite of the way I had seen things before this blessed miracle. And now again I do not know where to start to tell of God without beginning.

He reached out His hand to me in my fatal plunge into the depths of darkness and drew me up to the place where I could glimpse the Light of His Kingdom. When this time-less vision faded I found myself in a half-way state – I could still see the Light, but in the distance, as it were, and at the same time clearly remembered and still felt in myself the darkness of non-existence. And I was appalled by my old life, and my soul reached out towards the holy Light and gave herself over to tears of repentance.

There began a blessed period of my re-creation at the hands of God. Blessed, but terrifying: my whole life-style fell apart. My entire way of thinking was changed: I saw everything differently. I lost interest in my former circle of acquaintances. Art itself, which up to then had been the most important factor in my life as the means to knowledge of the world through contemplation of its visible aspect and wonder before its mysterious beauty, seemed to me to be limited and of little use in my search for absolute being. The old things collapsed – much that had seemed noble and great in the past now appeared naïve or, more often, 'an abomination'[vi] – to be replaced by unbridled prayer which

[iv] cf. Luke ii: 19.
[v] John viii: 23.
[vi] cf. Luke xvi: 15.

bore me into other spheres of Being. Prayer, not without a struggle, broke my former bonds, with painting especially, and continued for months before I was given the possibility of leaving the world and going to the Holy Mountain. There, in that blessed place, prayer took possession of me to an even greater degree.

The immensity of the task set before us by Christ should not deter – on the contrary, it ought to inspire us. Our Creator knows better than we do the ultimate possibilities of our nature. And if the Gospel Revelation speaks of our being chosen in Christ 'before the foundation of the world,'[vii.] which was clearly accepted by John, Paul, Peter and the other Apostles and Fathers, why should we be daunted by the one appeal worthy of attention, in comparison with which all other aims and ideas pale into insignificance? 'Many are called, but few are chosen.'[viii.] God addresses the call to all of us but the response depends on us.

Of course, we are no bolder than the Apostles who were stunned and afraid as they followed Christ on His way to Jerusalem, there to be condemned to a shameful death.[ix.] Once again the Lord said, 'I came not to send peace, but a sword'[x.] and 'division'.[xi.] Our own experience convinces us that the Lord has cast us into the tremendous conflict between belief and unbelief, and it is a terribly unequal fight – our hands and feet are tied, and we dare not strike with fire or steel. Our weapons are 'the sword of the Spirit, which is the word of God'[xii.] and love. This is indeed a holy war, which we, too, have chosen. Our fight is with the common enemy – death. Battling for our personal resurrection, we at

[vii.] Eph. i: 4.
[viii.] Matt. xxii: 14; xx: 16.
[ix.] cf. Mark x: 32–33.
[x.] Matt. x: 34.
[xi.] Luke xii: 51.
[xii.] Eph. vi: 17.

the same time wrestle for the universal rising again of all who have lived in the world since the beginning of time.

The Lord justified and hallowed His forefathers in the flesh. Likewise each one of us, if we follow Christ's commandments, can with tears of repentance restore the Divine Image in ourselves, which is clouded over, and thereby justify ourselves in our personal being, and assist in the justification of the generations that preceded us. We all of us bear in ourselves the fate of all mankind: it goes far beyond the bounds of earthly history and changes the course of cosmic life, for the world was created for such beings. When for the sake of a 'pottage of lentiles'[xiii] people refuse the path indicated by Christ − divinisation by the power of the Holy Spirit and the adoption of sons to the Eternal Father − the whole point of man's appearance in the world vanishes.

'A man is born into the world.'[xiv] For why?

No one could ever know God, or man, fully, as it is given us to know through Christ. He made manifest to us both the Heavenly Father and man as he was intended before the creation of the world. The Lord Jesus is absolute ontological Truth. It is only possible to know this Truth by following the method He Himself prescribed. 'Verily, verily, I say unto you, If a man keep my saying, he shall never see death' . . . 'If a man love me he will keep my words; and my Father will love him, and we will come unto him, and make our abode with him.'[xv]

'We know that the greater the love, the greater the sufferings of the soul,' said Staretz Silouan. The man to whom it has been given to feel Christ-like love is aware that such love moves the heart to wish everyone well, without exception.

[xiii] Gen. xxv: 33–34.
[xiv] John xvi: 21.
[xv] John viii: 51; John xiv: 23.

Such love is a life-giving fire. It is uncreated Light, and streams of energy beneficial for all mankind pour forth from him who possesses it. When it penetrates us it makes us Christ-like, and as it were naturally includes us in the sufferings of His love, which cannot bear to see man deprived of the highest good.

It is a sad thing that most people live their lives without aspiring as they should to become communicants in the Uncreated Light. Worse — when they hear tell of this Light, they do not believe in it: they even think that it does not exist, and consider anyone who has received this gift to be mentally sick. But the soul to whom it has been given to live the love of Christ knows how it leads the spirit into heavenly spheres, where death is not and God is contemplated in indescribable Light.

Logically there is no proving the possibility for us of eternal life. But when Divine strength descends on a man, he becomes a real participant in Divine eternity, and all rational proofs are superfluous.

Eternal life is existence of another order. Strictly speaking, it is God Himself; His Being, without beginning, touches us, fills us, and we, it can be said, are eternal in so far as we are in God.

Thus, it seems absolutely clear to us that all those who for whatever reason reject Christ do not know What and Whom they are rejecting.

Jesus Christ is the wisdom of God, the hidden wisdom, which God ordained before the world . . . which none of the princes and servants of this world knew.[xvi] Before Him the whole world, all its peoples, walked in dark ignorance of the way leading to the Kingdom of God and our Father. Now these hidden mysteries are revealed to us. We are given

[xvi] cf. I Cor. i:24; ii:7–8.

the surest knowledge of the ultimate meaning of our coming into this life. The Lord spoke to us of the pre-eternal love of the Father for us, and in Himself made manifest to us the Father as He is. But we in our mad folly crucified Him; and when He was hanging on the cross we mocked Him. And to this day continue to scoff.

V

The Rôle of FATHER-CONFESSOR
[from the Notes of a Spiritual Father on Mt. Athos]

Divine Providence – surprisingly, inscrutably – placed me in circumstances which meant that over a long period I was witness to the spiritual life of many an ascetic on the Holy Mountain. (A number of them were disposed to reveal to me matters which they surely did not speak of to other people.) I was deeply moved to come upon God's elect behind their humble appearance. Sometimes they themselves, preserved by God, did not realise the rich blessing that enveloped them. First and foremost it was given to them to perceive their own short-comings – at times to such an extent that they somehow did not presume even to imagine that God dwelt in them, and they in Him. A number of them were led to contemplation of the Uncreated Light without recognising its spiritual reality, partly because they were little acquainted with the works of the Holy Fathers describing this form of grace. Their ignorance protected them from any possible vainglory. In keeping with the custom for the Orthodox monastic confessor I did not explain what in fact the Lord was bestowing on them. To foster an ascetic's piety one must talk to him in such a way that his heart and mind are humbled – otherwise any further ascent is halted. I remember how Staretz Anatol on Old Russikon exclaimed to the young Silouan, 'If you are like this now, what will you be when you are an old man!'[i] In saying this, Anatol

[i] *The Monk of Mount Athos* by Archimandrite Sophrony, p. 25.

for many a year cast Silouan into fiery temptation. True, Silouan emerged victorious but at a bitter price. The power of the vision of God granted to him transcended the dynamism of the assaults of the enemy, and he issued from his exceptional spiritual battle enriched as were only a few in the whole history of the Church, and he left for our instruction his message regarding the difference between ascetic humility and the 'indescribable humility of Christ'. But for him, too, the risk of downfall was great, as it is for every Christian, every human being in general. Pride is the root of spiritual disaster. Through pride we become like demons. Humble love is natural to God, bringing redemption for them that are fallen away from the Kingdon of the Heavenly Father.

A confessor must sense the rhythm of the interior world of each and every man who turns to him. With this aim he prays the Divine Spirit to guide and inspire him to give the necessary counsel to each.

The work of a spiritual father is both a dread and a fascinating one. Painful but inspiring. He is a 'labourer together with God.'[ii] His is fecund work of the highest order, of incomparable honour – creating gods for eternity in the uncreated Light. In all things, of course, Christ is his example.[iii] Here is Christ's teaching:

'Verily, verily, I say unto you, The Son can do nothing of himself, but what he seeth the Father do: for what things soever he doeth, these also doeth the Son likewise. For the Father loveth the Son, and sheweth him all things that himself doeth; and he will shew him greater works than these, that ye may marvel. For as the Father raiseth up the dead, and quickeneth them, even so the Son quickeneth whom he will.'[iv]

It is enormously difficult to find the right words in which

[ii] cf. I Cor. iii:9.
[iii] John xiii: 15.
[iv] John v: 19–21.

to communicate spiritual conditions to the listener. It is vital that the confessor himself should have personal experience of, if possible, the whole gamut of spiritual states concerning which he ventures to speak to others. In his *Counsel to a Spiritual Pastor* St. John of the Ladder says this: 'The spiritual guide is he who has received from God, and through his own ascetic striving, such spiritual strength that he is able to rescue the storm-tossed soul from the very depths . . . The true teacher is he who has received directly from God the volume of spiritual wisdom traced in the mind by the Divine finger − that is, through the action of enlightenment − and has no need of other tomes . . . It ill befits teachers to recommend precepts taken from the works of others . . . If you are going to instruct the lowly, you must first study that which is on High . . . For the earthly cannot heal the earthly.'[v]

It was this very admonition that was given to me when I embarked on the ascetic struggle of spiritual service. Intrinsically, this envisages the begetting of God's word in the heart through prayer. Thus, when someone told St. Seraphim of Sarov that he had second sight, he replied that it was not so at all but that while he was talking to the penitent he prayed, and the first idea that came into his heart he accepted as coming from God.

Hearing confessions is awesome work, because if people come to the priest in the hope of clearly learning God's will, and instead of that, the priest offers advice of his own, which may not be pleasing to God, he thereby puts the penitents on the wrong track and does harm. St. Seraphim again said that when he spoke his own thoughts, mistakes could occur. And Blessed Staretz Silouan once added in a discussion on the subject that the 'mistakes' might not be fearful but they could be extremely consequential, such as he himself suffered from at the beginning of his monastic life.

Conscious of how far I was from due perfection, I myself

[v] Chapter 1:2 *et seq.*

prayed the Lord long and painfully not to let me blunder: to keep me in the ways of His real will, to inspire me with the right words for my brethren. And in the course of confession I would try to keep my mind alert in my heart, in order to detect God's thinking, and often even the words in which to convey it.

Investigation of the sacred principle of Orthodox tradition in practice is incredibly difficult. People, educated people, cling to a different starting-point – their own understanding. Every word the priest utters is simply that of another human being, and so subject to scrutiny. Blindly to comply with the spiritual father's injunctions would appear absurd to them. What the spiritual man discerns and accepts is rejected by the pragmatist because the latter lives on a different plane.[vi] I myself, when I remember people who are guided by their own impulses and who reject the counsel that the priest has received through prayer, refuse to solicit God to reveal to them His holy and all-perfect will. Thus I do not place them in a situation of conflict with God, merely telling them my own personal opinion, which may be reinforced by reference to the works of the Holy Fathers or the Holy Scriptures. I do not cause them to be impious – I allow them the right, as it were, sinlessly to refuse my advice as being merely that of another man. This, to be sure, is far from what we seek from the sacraments of the Church.

In these days of mass apostasy from Christianity the priestly function becomes more and more difficult. In his striving to extract people from the hell which their own contradictory passions have created, he constantly finds himself up against the death that has befallen them. The very feeling of time takes on a strange character – now tediously slow, now apparently non-existent, in the absence of any intelligent purpose.

[vi] cf. I Cor. ii: 10, 13.

It is impossible to understand people. Either they are blind and 'know not what they do,'[vii] or they suffer from spiritual and mental daltonism. Often they see things in diametrically-opposed lighting, like a photographic negative. Like this, it is impossible for them to discover the actual reality of life, and their condition leaves no room for any word of counsel. They are hostile to any impulse of godly love. Patient humility they consider to be hypocrisy. Any disposition to help them must spring from petty self-interest. The Christian spirit of not rendering evil for evil[viii] encourages them almost to insolence and they affront the clergy unwarrantably, attributing designs to them that had never occurred to them, mercilessly humiliating them and accusing them of arrogance. Their whole *ambiance* is ill-suited to the presence of a priest, whom they yet criticise if he declines contact in such circumstances. And so on, and so on.

I thank God Who opened up this enigma to us. The Lord forewarned us by His teaching, guided us by His example. And were it not so, we should fall into utter despair. A bishop wholly devoted to helping the suffering, who rescued many souls from inner and outer catastrophe, once wrote to me: 'I have come to fear love.' Some time later on I came to understand what he was saying. He meant that people who were helped by him attached themselves to him, and at first were of assistance to him in his sacred office. But later on, become self-confident and indispensable, they encroached upon his independence and made difficulties when he wanted to turn his attention to newcomers. At the time I received his letter I did not understand the dreadful significance of his words, which became clear to me afterwards, when I was serving as a priest in Europe. More than once was I reminded, and still am, of his paradoxical words: 'I have come to fear love.'

[vii] Luke xxiii: 34.
[viii] cf. I Thess. v: 15.

But at the same time there is another aspect to our mission. People relate to a priest in the same way as they do to God – carelessly rejecting Him as superfluous, yet taking for granted that the moment they need Him, they will call on Him, and He will be back. 'Father, forgive them, for they know not what they do.'

In France, having arrived from Greece, I met with the sort of people I had become unfamiliar with during my twenty-two years on the Holy Mountain – especially during the latter period when I was spiritual confessor to several hundred monks representing every aspect of the ascetic life on Mt. Athos. I make no secret of the fact that I was completely disorientated. The psychology of the monks, their patience and stamina, so far excelled all and everything that I encountered in Europe that I simply could not find either words or outward forms for contact. What monks accept gratefully, in Europe shattered people. Many of them spurned me, considering me abnormally hard-hearted, a distortion, even, of the Gospel spirit of love. And I concluded that the 'norms' of monastic ascetics and those of people of Western culture differed profoundly. There can be no doubt that the most 'abnormal' of all, both for the world of the 'Great Inquisitor' and of our own contemporaries, would be Christ. Who can hear Christ, or even more follow Him? What monks acquired after decades of weeping, our contemporaries think to receive after a brief interval – sometimes even in a few hours of pleasant 'theological' discussion. Christ's words – His every word – came to this world from on High. They belong to a sphere of other dimensions and can be assimilated only by means of prolonged prayer with much weeping. Otherwise, they will continue incomprehensible to man, however 'educated' he be, even theologically. Someone once said to me: 'Weighed down by the incomprehensible, one suffocates.' Yes, we are all, every one of us, stricken when we try our utmost to understand Christ's word. The Lord Himself said: 'Whosoever shall fall on this stone shall be broken: but on whomsoever it shall fall, it will grind him to powder.'[ix] Encountering this constituent of Christ's word, we gradually comprehend that it opens up to us the eternal spheres of the unoriginate Spirit. And then everything in us that resists Christ's word, we sense like the presence of death in us. And so, we carry on in a state of profound dichotomy – on the one hand, gratitude like a sweet pain pierces us to the heart; on the other, we feel unbearable shame for ourselves, and are appalled at the remoteness of our goal.

Both constant striving towards the Light of Christ and determination to endure all the consequences of this striving here on earth are imperative for every Christian. Only then do we reach understanding of the Gospel word – but we cannot observe how this happens because we are concerned with the real presence of God with us which is indescribable.

In every other sphere of human culture it is possible to observe 'progress' but this is not so in our life. Often the Holy Spirit withdraws from us because of one or another impulse of our heart, or perhaps a thought. But this withdrawal may occur because the Spirit sees us relaxed and content with what we have received or attained, and so retires, in order to show us how far distant we still are from what we ought to be.

It is not at all easy for a monk to bear the burden of being a confessor. On the one hand it is *beneficial* for him personally when people think poorly of him, since censure fosters humility. More urgent prayer rises to God from the ailing heart. It is easier for him to cry to God for the salvation of the world, since he himself exists by suffering, like the suffering of the great majority of the inhabitants of the earth. On the other hand, if he is engaged in the work of a spiritual father, every negative word about him instils distrust in him

[ix] Matt. xxi : 44.

on the part of people in need of exhortations, comfort and support. His sorrow is twofold: for himself as being unworthy of his calling, and then for the harm brought on the whole Church, on all mankind, when the authority of the priest is undermined. Unheeding a spiritual father's injunctions is tantamount to rejecting the word of Christ Himself. ('He that heareth you heareth me; and he that despiseth you despiseth . . . him that sent me.'[x.])

It is vitally important that priests and bishops should have the most genuine mutual respect and deference; that they should stop accusing each other, struggling for supremacy and envying superior talents. Even if one or the other servant of the Church exhibits certain shortcomings (and who is perfect?), it is better to encourage the penitent to have confidence in the priests who are available to them, either geographically or for other reasons. The very fact of being trusted will inspire a priest to utter true counsel. We know from the Lord's own words that unworthy men 'sat in Moses' seat',[xi.] yet Christ enjoined the people to observe and do whatsoever they bid, without emulating their way of life or their works.

Staretz Silouan did not have a settled spiritual father during all the years of his monastic life. He turned to whoever was at hand and available at the particular moment. He would pray beforehand that the Lord would be favourable unto him, and through the confessor grant him remission of sins and healing for his soul.

When I am dealing with the sick my attention concentrates on their spiritual state: whether they know God and do they trust in Him? Their sufferings, their pain and even life's catastrophes recede into the background.

However trifling their cause may seem, a man's woes

[x.] Luke x: 16.
[xi.] cf. Matt. xxiii: 2.

cannot be ignored. Often – too often even – the source of
people's misery lies in their indefatigable pursuit of sinful
pleasures. Even in such instances the confessor has only one
thing in mind – how best to heal this soul that has approached
him. The slightest incident may occasion acute pain to the
destitute and overburdened, and the priest's prayer is directed
to the heart of the suffering. Sympathy for every form of
human grief naturally evokes prayer in the confessor's soul.
And it is characteristic of the servant of Christ to see this
preoccupation with the pleasures of the flesh as the root-
cause of all the distress and difficulties of the universe. The
sufferings of the whole world accumulate in his heart, and
he prays with sorrowful tears for each and every man.

Contact on the Holy Mountain with monks who were ill
was considerably easier than were encounters with the sick
after my return to Europe. Monks are inwardly inclined
towards God, and everything is translated on to the spiritual
plane, whereas in Europe the psychological stresses prevail –
which compels the priest to show interest on that level also,
if he is to help people. Sitting at their bedside it would
sometimes happen that I entered into their sufferings, in
spirit, mentally and even physically, so that my body, too,
prayed for them. It did not occur often but there were cases
when God heard my prayers and fulfilled my petition.

It is still not clear to me why less intense prayer on my
part might occasionally cause the illness to take a favourable
turn, whereas at other times more profound supplication
brought no visible improvement.

I noticed that if in the course of prayer for someone the
grief in my heart resolved into peace and joy, that was always
a sure sign that my prayer had been heard, and healing
granted.

I did not seek the gift of being able to heal physical
illnesses. When praying for the sick I would commit all
things to the will of God, Who knows what each man needs
for his salvation. I am not at all convinced that this avoidance
on my part of any personal presence caused my prayers to

be ineffectual. I had no wish whatever to be a 'miracle-worker' — the idea alarmed me. And yet, contrariwise, so to speak, there were occasions — when prayer bore no fruit and left the believer saddened — when the thought would occur that it is vital for priests to have confirmation from God that He hears their prayers and fulfils their petitions. Upgrowth of help for those who pray for help through a priest would strengthen the faith of many in the Church. Moreover, the Lord Himself prayed to the Father: 'Father . . . glorify thy Son, that thy Son also may glorify thee.'[xii.]

It is more often in prayer for the living that our heart finds grief transformed into joy. But something similar occurs also with prayer for the dead — even the long ago dead. It is a wonderful experience to meet in spirit with souls long since departed, whom we may not even have known when they were alive. Such contact with the other world occurs particularly in prayer to the saints. But it can happen, too, though not often, in prayer for the departed, whether we knew them or not, that the heart is informed of their condition, be it good or bad. Real unity in the Holy Spirit with the souls of people who died recently or hundreds of years ago testifies to their personal immortality in our God. The encounter of our love with the love of them who are in our mind in the hour of prayer 'imparts unto us some spiritual gift, to the end we may be established.'[xiii.]

People like darkness, wherein lies death, and reject the light which is life, both temporal and eternal. If the priest has a heart that loves God's people, his soul is filled with compassion when he finds it impossible to communicate to them the light which is life. I have more than once dwelt on the strange aspect of spiritual service. And this is natural since it accompanies the confessor during the whole time of his mission. 'Death worketh in us, but life in you,' wrote St.

[xii.] John xvii: 1.
[xiii.] cf. Rom. i: 11–12.

96

Paul to the Corinthians.[xiv] Nor is this all: because they carry the light of life many people detest the servants of Christ, as before us they hated the Lord Himself: 'If the world hate you, ye know that it hated me before it hated you . . . Remember the word that I said unto you, The servant is not greater than his lord. If they have persecuted me, they will also persecute you; if they have kept my saying, they will keep your's also.'[xv]

When people talk to their spiritual father about their visions, his first consideration is to discover the true source of the vision – was it verily bestowed from on High, or merely the fruit of fantasy, or the influence of hostile spirits? The problem is sometimes a difficult one, and crucial. If we ascribe to the enemy something that comes from God we risk blaspheming against the Holy Ghost.[xvi] And vice versa: if we take demoniacal activity as proceeding from God, we push the penitent who is making his confession to us into worshipping demons. This makes it imperative for every spiritual father without exception to pray unceasingly, in general and on every separate occasion, that the Lord Himself preserve him from drawing the wrong conclusion.

When the state of affairs is unclear to the spiritual confessor, he can fall back on the psychological practice – suggest that the penitent be wary of peculiar phenomena of whatever sort. If the vision had really come from God, then humility would prevail in the penitent's soul, and he would readily accept the counsel not to get excited. Inversely, we may meet with a negative reaction and the urge to show that the vision could only have come from God. This may afford some grounds for doubt. Of course, the procedure is nothing more than a palliative and must not be adopted carelessly. Experience has shown that when someone puts temptation

[xiv] II Cor. iv: 12.
[xv] John xv: 18, 20.
[xvi] cf. Matt. xii: 28–31.

in the way of his fellow, he thereby provokes irritation and distress.

The same commandments have been given to every one of us, from which we may conclude that all men are equal in the sight of the Lord. Ascent to the top rung, to 'the measure of the stature of the fulness of Christ,'[xvii.] is barred to none. In the coming age the hierarchy of this world, both ecclesiastical and social, may find themselves overturned: 'God hath chosen the foolish things of the world to confound the wise; and . . . the weak things of the world to confound the things which are mighty; And base things of the world, and things which are despised . . . and things which are not, to bring to nought things that are.'[xviii.]

Spiritual 'elders' need not necessarily be priests or monks. The history of the Russian Church demonstrates this in the 18th and 19th centuries when numerous ascetics, endowed with grace, shunned priesthood and monasticism, in order to preserve their freedom for asceticism outside the control of officially-constituted organs. This sad phenomenon, injurious to the whole life of the Church, did not always originate in any anarchic attitude to the principle of priesthood itself. From the many books about such heroes of the spirit it is easy to see that great numbers of them were extremely God-fearing people who had been found worthy of manifest blessings and gifts from on High. Their way of life did not stimulate goodwill either on the part of the hierarchy or the civil powers and official organisations. Avoidance of the priesthood and monasticism was further interpreted by some to mean that so soon as a man donned the monastic habit, each and everyone assumed the right to pass judgment on the servants of Christ – judgment in an overwhelming total of instances that was iniquitous, hostile, defamatory. The more particularly endowed were very fre-

[xvii.] Eph. iv: 13.
[xviii.] I Cor. i: 27, 28; I Cor. xv: 24–28.

quently even subject to harsh persecution because their way of living exceeded the understanding of those at the helm of power. The history of our Church overflows with such instances, and there is no need to name them individually.

Shifts from one state to another – often from acute suffering to profound joy, from despair to contemplation and inspired hope, from prolonged weeping to sweet peace, and so on – are natural to one who prays long and fervently. Much and persistent prayer, together with abstinence in all things, refines perception – the soul becomes like the most sensitive hearing-aid, instantly reacting to the faintest sound, even to an inaudible stirring in the air. And when our spirit has hundreds of times repeated the same cycle of rise and fall, the soul so assimilates both states that she continually lives both heaven and hell within her. This may seem paradoxical to many but in fact it is an indication of increasing love – an approaching to likeness to Christ. Here is St. Paul writing of himself: 'Who is weak, and I am not weak? who is offended, and I burn not?'[xix.] And he bade the Romans: 'Rejoice with them that do rejoice, and weep with them that weep.'[xx.] According to the pastoral principle of the Fathers – one must not urge one's flock to try for what one has not achieved oneself. I do not think that St. Paul in this respect was less strict than the Fathers. Approach to the confessor of souls in trouble cannot be regimented or arbitrarily organised. It is impossible to appoint set hours – one time for hearing people in trouble and another for those who feel joyous. This means that every pastor must at all times be ready to weep with them that weep and rejoice with the joyous . . . to despond with them that are in despair and restore to faith those that have gone astray. But here, too, as all through our life, the Lord Himself is our paramount model. We see from the Gospels and especially from His last

[xix.] II Cor. xi: 29.
[xx.] Rom. xii: 15.

days and hours how He lived at one and the same time the fulness − unattainable for us − both of suffering and of triumphant victory: both death and Divine glory. 'Ye know that after two days is the feast of the passover, and the Son of man is betrayed to be crucified'[xxi.] . . . 'I will not drink henceforth of this fruit of the vine, until that day when I drink it *new with you in my Father's kingdom.*'[xxii.] . . . 'My God, my God, why hast thou forsaken me?'[xxiii.] 'Verily I say unto thee, *To day shalt thou be with me in paradise*'[xxiv.] . . . 'and his sweat was as it were great drops of blood falling down to the ground'[xxv.] . . . 'Father, forgive them; for they know not what they do'[xxvi.] . . . 'My soul is exceeding sorrowful, even unto death.'[xxvii.] 'Art thou the Christ, the Son of the Blessed? And Jesus said, I am: and ye shall see the Son of man sitting on the right hand of power, and coming in the clouds of heaven.'[xxviii.]

And if we really do Christ's bidding, all that He went through will be repeated in us, be it to a lesser degree. The intensity of Christ's suferings cannot be gauged. Entering into them makes it possible for us to know the eminence of Divine providence for us and achieve the perfection of love. After death our sufferings will cease to be fatal, as may happen with us in our worldly state: they will no longer be able to injure our *new life*, so abundantly granted to us, our inheritance that cannot be taken away. The spirit of man retains the capacity to suffer with all who are deprived of Divine glory − genuinely suffer − but this will be merely one of the many different manifestations of all-embracing love − death has no power over those who are redeemed in

---

[xxi.] Matt. xxvi: 2.
[xxii.] Matt. xxvi: 29.
[xxiii.] Matt. xxvii: 46.
[xxiv.] Luke xxiii: 43.
[xxv.] Luke xxii: 44.
[xxvi.] Luke xxiii: 34.
[xxvii.] Matt. xxvi: 38.
[xxviii.] Mark xiv: 61−62.

Christ. Here on earth spiritual torment sometimes drives us to the threshold of death; but often in answer to prayer strength abundant descends on us and restores what has been destroyed – sometimes even intensifying the life energy in us. If we were even to a tiny degree capable of entering into the Mother of God's measureless grief as she stood by the cross, it would be clear to us that without help from on High the earthly body could not bear such suffering. But the love of the Holy Spirit, abiding with her since the day of the Annunciation, prevailed over deathly pain – she stayed alive, and saw her Risen Son taken up to heaven, and from the Father sending down the Holy Spirit on the Church born in His blood.

Anyone acquainted with the history of Christ's Church knows the labour involved century after century to express such dogmatic knowledge, be it of God or of the Church herself, that would be a safeguard against the various forms of deviation disfiguring the spiritual life of her members personally and of the Church as a whole.

Supported by age-old experience, we naturally believe that the way is open to every member of the Church to the most perfect degree possible on earth and in heaven of knowledge of God. And this indepedently of any social origin or hierarchical status. Let us consider, for example, instances nearest to us in time – St. Seraphim Sarovsky or Staretz Silouan, Metropolitan Philaret of Moscow or John of Kronstadt. We could go back to the very beginning of our Church – to the Apostles, who were poor fishermen. And if it were otherwise, we should have to make such ascents into the Divine spheres dependent on human schooling. The Lord demonstrated in Himself that God the Father is often closer to 'little ones' and the unfortunate. 'The seventy [disciples] returned again with joy, saying, Lord, even the devils are subject unto us through thy name. And he said unto them, I beheld Satan as lightning fall from heaven. Behold, I give unto you power to tread on serpents and scorpions, and over all the power of the enemy: and nothing shall by any means hurt you. Notwithstanding in this rejoice not, that the spirits are subject unto you; but rather rejoice, because your names are written in heaven. In that hour Jesus rejoiced in spirit, and said, I thank thee, O Father, Lord of heaven and earth, that thou hast hid these things from the wise and prudent, and hast revealed them unto babes: even so, Father; for so it seemed good in thy sight.' And turning to His disciples, He said 'All things are delivered to me of my Father: and no man knoweth who the Son is, but the Father; and who the Father is, but the Son, and he to whom the Son will reveal him.'[xxix.] 'And the Jews marvelled, saying, How knoweth this man letters, having never learned? Jesus answered them, and said, My doctrine is not mine, but his that sent me. If any man will do his will he shall know of the doctrine, whether it be of God, or whether I speak of myself [as man].'[xxx.]

Secular scholarship provides the means for expressing experience but without the assistance of grace cannot communicate really redemptive knowledge. Knowledge of God is existentialist, not abstract and intellectual. Countless numbers of professional theologians are awarded top diplomas yet in actual fact remain profoundly ignorant in the sphere of the Spirit. This is because they do not live according to Christ's commandments, and so are deprived of the light of knowledge of God. God is love – but love acquired by torturous repentance and fear of God. 'Be not afraid of them that kill the body, and after that have no more that they can do . . . Fear him, which after he hath killed hath power to cast into hell; yea, I say unto you, Fear him.'[xxxi.] The Fathers of our Church affirm that unless we go through the burning fire of the fear of God, Divine love does not move into the soul. This love will embrace all creation, uniting us with

[xxix.] Luke x: 17–22.
[xxx.] John vii: 15–17.
[xxxi.] Luke xii: 4–5.

the All-powerful Master, with the God of love. It is Light, a 'pearl of great price,'[xxxii.] incomparable. To lose this pearl is a dreadful thing for the soul. The nature of divine fear is indescribable, as are all things in our God. It is possible to picture the spiritual state of a human being as a 'nerve-centre' – faith in Christ is the beginning of love, though still pre-dawn Light. This faith induces profound repentance and a certain dread of forfeiting the treasure we have found – God, that is. Prayerful weeping of repentance cleanses our being, and hope is born. Hope, like a further degree of love towards God, increases our fear of not being vouchsafed eternal sojourn with Him. Every ascent of our spirit towards greater love increases fear. But when Christ's great love touches our heart and mind, then our spirit in the flame of this holy love will embrace all creation in compassionate love, and the feeling of transition into divine eternity acquires invincible strength. This event is mightier far than every other happening in the annals of the fallen world – God united in one with man.

Forgive me – it is beyond me to embody in words the 'abundance of life' vouchsafed to us in Christ. I do not see how it is possible to outline that marvellous labyrinth, with all its paradoxicalness, that makes up the heart of life. Here am I, I loathe myself as I am. With this self-hatred prayer becomes crazy, as it were, all-consuming, tearing me away from every material thing. It carries my spirit into light-bearing infinity, into indescribable depths. There I forget the bitter taste of my grievous self-hatred – all is transformed into love of God in total abstraction from self – a strange interweaving of love for God and hatred of self. There is fear, too, that devours but love heals this pain, and I forget all dread. But when our spirit returns from this feast of Divine love in Christ, the fear returns of being distanced from that Light, from that Life: will it not always be thus?

[xxxii.] Matt. xiii: 46.

The individual himself has no wish to return to this world but love towards God–Christ is part and parcel of love towards one's fellow-man. Living and functioning in everyday life is only possible if grace diminishes in us. If one is plunged deep in intense prayer, how converse with people engaged in arduous struggle for bread and a hearth, who are worried about family or matrimonial ties, business failures, or illness, their own or of those dear to them; and so on? You will not help a man if you ignore his primitive needs. The Christian mission entails loving compassion. One must either take into one's heart the difficulties and sorrow of those who turn to us or, alternatively, enter into their hearts, their torment — unite with them. This exposes one to the danger of starting a conflict with them, of being infected by their belligerence, becoming exasperated with their inconsistencies and intractability — often their hostility. One tries to help, to pass on to them sacred treasure, the fruit of years and years of weeping — and they are dissatisfied. Should one abandon them? Or agonise for them as did all the apostles and the pastors who succeeded them?

'In weariness and painfulness, in watchings often, in hunger and thirst, in fastings often, in cold and nakedness . . . that which cometh upon me daily, the care of all the churches. Who is weak, and I am not weak? who is offended, and I burn not?'[xxxiii] . . . And St. Paul again: 'So now also Christ shall be magnified in my body, whether it be by life, or by death. For to me to live is Christ, and to die is gain. But if I live in the flesh, this is the fruit of my labour: yet what I shall choose I wot not. For I am in a strait betwixt two, having a desire to depart, and to be with Christ; which is far better: Nevertheless to abide in the flesh is more needful for you. And having this confidence, I know that I shall abide and continue with you all for your furtherance and joy of faith.'[xxxiv]

[xxxiii] II Cor. xi: 27–29.
[xxxiv] Phil. i: 20–25.

Priests burdened with pastoral cares are similarly torn. On the one hand they know that there is no profit in gaining the whole world, and losing one's own soul.[xxxv.] On the other there is the Lord's injunction, 'Go ye [therefore], and teach all nations, baptizing them in the name of the Father, and of the Son, and of the Holy Ghost.'[xxxvi.] 'Freely ye have received, freely give.'[xxxvii.] Parallel with this goes the idea that the vital need for mankind is to KNOW THE TRUE GOD.[xxxviii.] But how are we to find Him? So then, if KNOWLEDGE of God is to continue on earth, it is imperative that people should not go astray like sheep without a shepherd. This knowledge is so important that St. Isaac of Syria makes a fearful statement, difficult to understand and painful to grasp: 'Do not liken them that work signs and wonders and powerful deeds in the world with them that elect to fast and pray in the desert. Prefer inner stillness rather than feeding the hungry in the world, and the conversion of many peoples to the worship of God.'

Prefer the apparent inaction of inner silence to feeding the hungry? There are two kinds of hunger – physical and spiritual. '. . . Behold, the days come, saith the Lord God, that I will send a famine in the land, not a famine of bread, nor a thirst for water, but of hearing the words of the Lord: And they shall wander from sea to sea, and from the north even to the east, they shall run to and fro to seek the word of the Lord, and shall not find it. In that day shall the fair virgins and young men faint for thirst. They that swear by the sin of Samaria, and say, Thy god, O Dan, liveth; and, The manner of Beer-sheba liveth; even they shall fall, and never rise up again.'[xxxix.] Now in our day we see dismay everywhere, and increasing despair. More books are pub-

---

[xxxv.] cf. Mark viii: 36.
[xxxvi.] Matt. xxviii: 19.
[xxxvii.] Matt. x: 8.
[xxxviii.] cf. John xvii: 3.
[xxxix.] Amos viii: 11–14.

lished than ever before but, alas, most of them are syncretic, attempting to conjoin heterogeneous elements into a single whole – elements in their very core contradictory and in practice incompatible. Thus our ever-increasing confusion. St. Isaac of Syria believed repentance and the silence of the anchorite to be a surer way to knowledge of God and life in Him. And it is just this – now so rare in the world – that for him was the most important thing of all. The loss of true knowledge of God – given to us by Christ and the Holy Spirit – would damage the whole world irreparably.

I have met many people who were going through a serious crisis on the plane of the spirit. In talking with them I would remember my own crisis which continued for years – years of maximum stress for me. When prayer won the battle in me I abandoned my artistic profession to enter the Theological Institute in Paris, where the students were serious and the professors of the requisite high standard. But prayer 'stifled' me day and night, and so I left the Institute to go to Mt. Athos, where the whole of life is concentrated on divine service and prayer. To attend courses on church matters was impossible for me, since to put my whole mind on the subjects being taught impaired my earlier total striving for God. I realised that if I hungered to know God, I would have to give myself to Him in a greater degree than I had devoted myself to my painting. Divine eternity enthralled me. All the same, on leaving France I took care to burn my boats so that, if I began to have doubts, I should not be able to return to my former life. I did have a moment of temptation – making my way from the sea up to the monastery, I was assailed by the thought: Here you are, volunteering for life imprisonment! And that was the one single occasion in my whole life when for an instant my heart hesitated. I am recalling it now though in the course of many decades I have never once looked back on the past. Ahead of me, far distant, lies what I seek, and only a few fleeting days are left to me. My soul has dried up among the vanities of this world, and

I need the living waters that proceed from my Creator and 'flow to life eternal'. I write, and all the time keep a hold on myself lest I use the sort of language which, in fact, is the only possible one to express the excruciating pain of my whole constitution, in my search for God my Saviour. My entire body likewise prayed, clenching tight into one. My forehead pressed to the floor, tears flowed in streams, burning, dissolving the flintstone of the passions. The sadness in my heart was heavier, went deeper, than any earthly loss could have caused. I tried to open myself up to God, totally. I besought Him not to reject me from before His Face; to grant me to recognise the true path to Him; to remove from me every delusion that might lead me astray. I recognised my baseness, my nastiness, ugliness, corruptness, and was enfeebled by seeing myself as I was. And my need to be healed by the strength of the Holy Spirit was like that of a young man avid for life and finding himself being mercilessly destroyed by some illness. God had revealed Himself to me before I enrolled in the Theological Academy. I arrived on Mt. Athos utterly convinced of the realness of the Son of God, Who alone could manifest His Father to me. But I was in hell – the Holy of Holies could never accept such vileness. And my clamour for regeneration on every plane of my being was a cry in the wilderness . . . I fear to say it, in a cosmic, not an earthly wilderness. And my anguish went beyond the boundaries of time.

What I went through, on the one hand helped me in my duties as a spiritual confessor, at first on the Holy Mountain, to the monks, then later in Europe to people of various ages, different mentalities and varying intellectual levels. On the other hand it led me into error – I thought that everyone aspired to God to the same degree, and in this I was mistaken. To judge by oneself is not always right.

I was deeply convinced of my spiritual poverty. Nevertheless, I could not refuse the task of confessor imposed on me. I certainly did not seek it – I may say that I wanted nothing in this world then, because my whole being strained towards God, against Whom I had so grievously sinned. Self-condemned, my mind lived in hell. Only for odd moments did the hostility of the fathers and brethren of the monastery upset me – in general, I was profoundly indifferent to my standing in this world or the attitude towards me of older and younger monks. Envy was foreign to me. No social or even hierarchical rank existed for me that could quench the fire consuming my soul. Maybe the presence in me of that fire irritated some of my brethren? Maybe because of the inflammation in me my demeanour was not quite customary. Who knows? It was just that with my whole might I required forgiveness from God and had no thought for anything else.

Not long before his demise Staretz Silouan quite unexpectedly said to me, 'When you become a spiritual confessor, do not refuse those who turn to you'. At that time I felt physically on my last legs, exhausted by malaria, a mild form of which harassed me throughout those years. I did not know how long I had to live, and so did not pay much attention to the Staretz' words. He does not realise, I thought, how ill I am. And inded, his behest did not stay long in my mind.

I remembered it four or five years later when, likewise unexpectedly, I was asked by Higoumen Archimandrite Seraphim to be confessor to their Monastery of St. Paul. Naturally, obedient to Staretz Silouan I made no objection and agreed to go to them on the day appointed.

The ascetic task of being a spiritual confessor radically altered my life – not making it more profound but causing me to lose grace. The integrality of my former strivings was infringed. Focussing attention on what was said to me in confession interrupted my concentration on my inner being. I knew that *there, within, was the beginning and there the end and the crowning. Thence the departure and thither the return.* Without concentrated prayer from the heart, beseeching God all the time for His word and blessing, the office of the spiritual confessor is in vain. Without constant enlightenment from on High even the Church would become another of the half-blind powers of this world, the conflicts between which bring destruction to the life of the universe. Wherein lies the task of the spiritual confessor? Painstaking concern for every individual, to help him enter the sphere of Christ's peace; to assist in people's inner rebirth and transfiguration through the grace of the Holy Spirit; to give courage to the faint-hearted to strive to live according to the Lord's commandments. In short, the spiritual education of each and everyone. A Serbian bishop[xl.] wrote admirably on this theme: What or whose image is being created in our contemporary schools? Which of these schools knows that man was made in the image of God without beginning? And He appeared on earth and was revealed to man; and now we know that true education consists in restoring to the descendants of Adam the image of Christ that was destroyed in the fall.

The spiritual confessor is bound by his calling always to pray for people close and far away. In this prayer he is plunged into a life novel for him. In praying for those in despair over the insuperable difficulties of the struggle for existence, he worries and feels anxiety for them. Praying for the sick, he senses their fear in the face of death. Praying for those in hell (the hell of the passions), he himself experiences that infernal state. All of this he lives inside himself, as his own torment. But in reality it is not he himself – he merely takes on the burdens of other people. In the first instant he does not understand what is happening – why is it that again and even more than before he is attacked by passions, many of which he did not know in the past? Only later does he discover that he has been brought into other people's battle for life; that his prayer has met with the spiritual reality of those for whom he prays to God. He is overwhelmed by the breath of death that strikes the human race. Both his personal and liturgical prayer take on cosmic dimensions. The struggle for the life of those entrusted to him by Providence is some-times of short duration – a few words from the heart to the

<hr />

[xl.] Bishop Nikolai Velimirovich.

God of love. But it can continue for a long time. Though he surrenders his own life, the spiritual confessor is still not entirely free from the passions. He prays for others as for himself, since their life has now merged with his. He repents for himself and for them. He prays for remission of sins for all of us. His repentance becomes repentance for the whole world, for all mankind. In this impulse of his spirit there is a likeness to Christ, Who took upon Himself the sins of the world. It is a difficult prayer – one never sees the sought-for outcome. The world on the whole spurns it.

Prayer of repentance is an indescribably marvellous gift to us from the Heavenly Father. 'Then opened he their understanding, that they might understand the scriptures, And said unto them, Thus it is written, and thus it behoved Christ to suffer, and to rise from the dead the third day: And that repentance and remission of sins should be preached in his name among all nations . . .'[xli]

The principle of Christ's preaching – 'Repent: for the kingdom of heaven is at hand'[xlii] – we have lost sight of. Clearly it was nothing less than the continuation of something that began in Eden – of the conversation betwen God and man.[xliii] Called upon by God to repent, Adam and Eve refused to acknowledge their iniquity. Eve pusillanimously accused the serpent, while Adam brazenly laid the blame on Eve and on God Himself for giving him such a wife.

Slowly century followed century. In the course of their tedious procession mankind came to recognise the consequences of the rupture with God the Father. Souls appeared on the scene, by diverse sufferings prepared for a measure of communion with God. Then the world was given the Sinaitic Revelation. Through the Law of Moses the chosen people

---

[xli] Luke xxiv: 45–47.
[xlii] Matt. iv: 17.
[xliii] cf. Gen. iii: 8 *et seq.*

lived before the Face of the Unseen Almighty God, and grew in spirit to be capable of further reconciliation with Him. And then there appeared in the flesh He Who conversed with Adam and Eve on the day that started the tragic history of mankind. Thus our direct contact with the Person of the Creator of the world was restored, that had been interrupted for centuries.

The Lord disclosed to us the mysteries of Divine Being and created life. But all his 'work'[xliv.] is so grandiose that our mind's eye cannot take it in in detail, and our heart lacks the energy to embrace His miracles. In his Easter message St. John Chrysostom says, 'Hell was vexed, for it was overturned. It took a body but met with God. It adopted earth, and encountered heaven. It took that which was seen, and fell upon the unseen'. That is exactly what happens with us when we decide to follow Jesus Christ. We see a man in his created flesh but in reality He is God. We contemplate Him as, resistless, He submits to an unjust death but we recognise in Him our Creator and Saviour. We hear our everyday language coming from His lips but it opens up to us the eternity of Absolute Being.

The more fully our spirit strives after Jesus the Nazarene, the more striking becomes the contrast between His heavenly world and the visible reality of our universe. One of the first consequences of the primordial Fall was fratricide. And ever since then that sin has been the principal sin throughout history. The nature of man as a whole was torn to shreds — people, meeting with their like, do not recognise themselves, do not see our common unity of life. Struggling for their own individual existence, they slay their fellows, not understanding that thereby they plunge themselves into death in common with them. Baneful passion has ousted the bonds of love in people's souls, and the urge to repress one's neighbour for the sake of a comfortable life for oneself and one's

[xliv.] cf. John xvii: 4.

offspring. Because of this benightedness our whole world is plunged in an ocean of blood, a hostile atmosphere, a nightmare of mutual destruction. The sin of our forefathers brought about universal dissolution. To this day mankind has not only failed to release itself from the spirit of fratricide but continues to plunge ever deeper into lethal delirium. The experience of centuries has taught man nothing. Victory through violence is always and inevitably short-term in this world. Translated into eternity, it will prove a never-ending disgrace.

'All ye are brethren', said the Teacher – Christ. 'One is your Father, which is in heaven.'[xlv.]

The Lord Jesus Christ – the greatest of miracles – came to earth to redeem us. But even Him we slaughtered. Yet the 'smiting of the Shepherd'[xlvi.] on the visible plane was an incomparable victory in the sphere of the eternal Spirit – a victory likewise in the sufferings of devoted love that brought everlasting fruit. Thus will it be also with them who follow in His steps. Those who love Christ will keep His Word and at the end of all things will turn out to be truly victorious and find their resting-place in His kingdom.[xlvii.]

To be a spiritual confessor in our times is a super-human task. It is difficult to find salvation in these days of mass apostasy. Christ's contemporaries 'came out with swords and staves to take him . . . but the Lord said to them, This is your hour, and the power of darkness.'[xlviii.] Has not this infernal 'darkness' thickened even more in our day? Despair never ceases to escalate for the inhabitants of our planet. One sheds blood, praying for this world as it is. Here is one of my prayers to the Most High God.

[xlv.] Matt. xxiii: 8–9.
[xlvi.] cf. Matt. xxvi: 31.
[xlvii.] cf. John xvi: 33.
[xlviii.] cf. Luke xxii: 52–53.

REVEAL Thy mysteries to my heart. Make manifest to me, a sinner, Thy Wisdom concealed since the beginning of time. By Thy Holy Spirit enlighten the eyes of my understanding, that I may perceive Thy good Providence for all manner of people even in the most dread happenings of our times. Give my soul the strength of patient love, for my frail flesh swoons at the sight of – and still more at hearing about – the unbearable torments inflicted all over the world on captive fellow creatures . . . Oft-times hast Thou given me confidence in the final victory of Thy Light, and yet – Thou seest I am far spent in my service.

Since my young days I have watched in sad bewilderment the scene unfolding before my eyes. But there have been hours of strange triumph when the extreme folly of it all assured me of the inevitable presence of another 'pole' in the existence of the world – Wisdom. I did not attain to this Wisdom but it would flood my soul with hope of transfiguration for all creatures, and prayer for the whole world would revive in my heart, and undying Light heal my soul.

In praying for people one's heart often senses their spiritual or emotional state. Because of this the spiritual father can experience their psychological state – contentment and happiness in love, exhaustion from over-work, fear of approaching hardship, the terror of despair, and so on. Remembering the sick before the Lord, in spirit he bends over the beds of millions of people at any moment looking into the face of death, and suffering agonies. Turning his attention to the dying, the priest naturally enters mentally into the other world, and participates either in the soul's tranquil going to God or her apprehension of the unknown which shocks the imagination prior to the actual moment of departure from this world. And if standing at the bedside of only one person dying in agony affords us a vision shattering in its contrast to our conception of the first-created man, the thought of all the suffering on earth is more than our psyche, even our body, can endure. For the priest—confessor this is a crucial threshold – what must he do? Shut his eyes on it all, obedient to the instinct for self-preservation natural to all of us? Or continue further? Without the preliminary ascetic effort of profound repentance, the gift from on High, this 'continuing' is beyond man. In actual fact it is already a question of following Christ to the Garden of Gethsemane and on to Golgotha, in order to live with Him, by His strength, the tragedy of the world as one's own *personal* tragedy; of, outside time and beyond space, embracing in spirit, with compassionate love, our whole human race bogged down in insoluble conflicts. The fact that we have forgotten, even rejected, our primordial calling lies at the heart of the universal tragedy. The all-destroying passion of pride can only be overcome by total repentance, through which the blessing of Christ-like humility descends on man, making us children of the Heavenly Father.

Not only our psycho-physical make-up refuses to enter into Christ's world-redeeming prayer and sacrifice of love – our spirit, too, quails before this reality, and our mind lacks the strength to rise 'up there', to the highest, spiritually, of all other mountains, where the Lord surrendered Himself into the hands of the Father. 'With men it is impossible, but not with God: for with God all things are possible.'[xlix] Rising 'thither' occurs without any preliminary idea concerning this event. The soul is lifted up, naturally, as it were, in her prayer of repentance for her sins, for her fall, which unites her through this state with all the preceding centuries of the history of mankind. And this happens suddenly, unexpectedly, unwittingly. In intense weeping over herself the soul, by the gift of the Holy Spirit, is led existentially into the essence of our sinning, into its metaphysical dimensions, as the fall from blessed, imperishable life in the Light pro-

[xlix] Mark x: 27.

ceeding from the Countenance of the Father of all. This is not philosophical contemplation, nor intellectual theologizing — it is a *fact* of our being: in the fall of Adam mankind spurned God. The really dreadful thing is that in our blindness we do not see our sin. Its nature begins to be revealed to us through faith in Christ-God.

'Jesus said, I go my way, and ye shall seek me, and shall die in your sins: whither I go, ye cannot come . . . Ye are from beneath; I am from above; ye are of this world; I am not of this world. I said therefore unto you, that ye shall die in your sins: for if ye believe not that I am he [that was revealed to Moses on Sinai], *ye shall die* in your sins. Then said they unto him, Who art thou? And Jesus saith unto them, Even the same that I said unto you from the beginning.'[i]

Thus we see that our personal sin is the sin of all mankind. And the priestly prayer for forgiveness of sins for the world is repentance for all mankind. Everyone who truly repents of his offences against the Father's love, by the power of this same God is borne into this sphere that is mysterious for us now. I am an insignificant being but I belong to the great body of mankind, and cannot detach myself from it. My sin — I at first live it as only my sin. But later on it becomes clear to me that it is *that selfsame sin* described in the Bible, in the Book of Genesis.[ii] I am of no account but what is taking place inside me is not insignificant — not worthless in the eyes of Him Who created me. Did He not 'empty' Himself to the utmost, give Himself over to humiliation that passes our understanding? This He did whilst in His nature continuing to be the infinitely great God. And He did so in order to save us.

For many a long year now I have been trying to persuade those who turn to me to apprehend the trials that befall

[i] John viii: 21–25.
[ii] Ch. iii.

them not only within the bounds of their individual existence but also as a revelation of how mankind lives and has lived in its millennium existence. Every experience, be it of joy, be it of pain, can bring us new knowledge vital for our salvation. When in ourselves we live the whole human world, all the history of mankind, we break out of the locked circle of our own 'individuality' and enter into the wide expanses of 'hypostatic' forms of being, conquering death and participating in divine infinity.

This amazing itinerary is unknown to all except the Christian. At first departure from the narrow prison of the individual can seem paradoxical: we ourselves feel crushed by our own sufferings – where shall we find the strength of spirit to embrace in compassion all the millions of people who at any given moment are suffering like us, and surely even more than we are? If we feel joyful, we can manage it better somehow but when we cannot cope with our own pain, sympathy for the multitudes only increases our already unbearable torment. Nevertheless, try this, and you will see how with the profound weeping of prayer for all suffering humanity energy will appear, of another order, not of this world. This new form of compassion, coming down from on High, differs from the first impulse shut tight inside oneself, in that now, instead of destroying, it quickens us. The horizons of our own individual life are immeasurably widened, and many passages in the Gospels and Epistles we can intepret as applicable to our own case – even what we might remark ourselves. For instance, 'Now no chastening for the present seemeth to be joyous, but grievous: nevertheless afterward it yieldeth the peaceable fruit of righteousness.'[lii] Or, '. . . Looking unto Jesus, the author and finisher of our faith; who for the joy that was set before him endured the cross, despising the shame, and is set down at

[lii] Heb. xii: 11.

the right hand of the throne of God . . .'[liii] By opening ourselves to greater suffering in spirit, we surmount our individual ordeal. Especially will it be like this at the end: death overcomes death, and the power of Resurrection prevails.

It is vital that we should all pray long and hard; that through years and years of fervent prayer – prayer of contrition, particularly – our fallen nature may be so transformed that it can assimilate the Unoriginate Truth made manifest to us. And this, before we depart from this world. Christ – Who showed this Truth to us in our flesh – draws us to Himself and calls us to follow after Him. Our eternal abiding with Him in the unshakeable Kingdom depends on our response to His summons. The measureless grandeur of the task set before us inspires heart and mind with fear – the fear of love, since we may prove utterly unworthy of God. Fear because we are confronted with painful ascetic effort – the kingdom of heaven suffereth *violence*.[liv] The battle is indescribable. 'Outer darkness'[lv] threatens those who are mastered by pride or base passions. On the other hand, 'To him that overcometh will I grant to sit with me in my throne, even as I also overcame, and am set down with my Father in his throne. He that hath an ear, let him hear what the Spirit saith.'[lvi]

We are faced with a mighty battle but an especial, holy battle, not like the fratricidal wars that crowd the history of our world ever since Cain killed his brother Abel. Our common and only real enemy is our mortality. We must grapple painfully with the death that pervades all things, first and foremost ourselves. The Lord's gospel belongs to another, higher, celestial plane, where everything is 'not after man, and not of

---

[liii] Heb. xii: 2.
[liv] Matt. xi: 12.
[lv] cf. Matt. viii: 12; xiii: 41–43.
[lvi] Rev. iii: 21–22.

man.'[lvii] It would be criminal to belittle its eternal dimensions – that would cancel its power of attraction and even meaning for people. Of course, Christ's commandments, 'Love your enemies . . . Be ye perfect, even as your Father which is in heaven is perfect' – surpass our mind and our strength. But Christ in our flesh manifested this perfection: 'He overcame the world'. Which means victory can be given to us, too, when we are with Him. Speaking of His word, Christ said, 'The seed is the word of God.'[lviii] May it be in us as seed not of this world. After death, having fallen in compatible soil, it will produce imperishable fruit.

[lvii] cf. Gal. i: 11–12.
[lviii] Luke viii: 11.

PART II

I

The JESUS PRAYER

Now in our day the Jesus Prayer is becoming known all over the world. Much that is written about it is worthy of serious attention but equally not a few absurd ideas are prevalent. This has decided me to pen a brief treatise on the subject in order, on the one hand, to warn devout enthusiasts concerning blind-alleys and, on the other, to confirm the basic theological and ascetic tenets of this important spiritual culture.

The theory of the Prayer can be set out in a few pages but its practical application to Christian ascetics demands such painful effort that from the earliest days the Fathers and teachers of the Church have counselled seekers after this form of union with God to approach it in fear, to look for guides experienced in this way of asceticism. I do not hope to cover all aspects of such a momentous matter. I shall limit myself to setting out something of what I myself was taught during my time on Mt. Athos, in the monastery and in the desert. (It will be quite impossible not to repeat what other writers have already written. But it seems to me that such repetition will not be superfluous – indeed, it may be vital in elucidating the subject in other contexts.)

In the last hours of His life with us the Lord said, 'Hitherto have ye asked nothing in my name: ask, and ye shall receive, that your joy may be full . . . Verily, verily, I say unto you, Whatsoever ye shall ask the Father in my name, he will give it you.'[i] These words of Christ's furnish both the dogmatic and ascetic foundation for the Jesus Prayer.

There can be no doubt that Christ's disciples observed this commandment and we can be even surer that they already knew the power of His Name when they were sent forth 'as sheep in the midst of wolves'[ii] to bring peace to the world, to heal the sick, to proclaim the coming of the Divine Kingdom. 'The seventy returned again with joy, saying, Lord, even the devils are subject unto us through thy name.'[iii] And on another occasion '. . . we saw one casting out devils in thy name.'[iv] Thus the history of the Jesus Prayer dates from apostolic times. The actual formula of the Prayer has not been preserved but the New Testament is full of instances when the Prayer effected many striking miracles.

But what does the Divine Name mean? In order to pray 'in the Name of' is it necessary to understand its significance, its nature, its essence? Yes, indeed, it is even vital if our joy is to be full.[v]

The depths of life in Christ are bottomless, to be assimilated by a long process demanding all our strength. The content and meaning of the Divine Name are revealed only gradually. Occasional repetition of it may also rejoice and be dear to the heart. But we must not stop half-way. Our time here is brief and every hour must be made use of that our knowledge of God may grow. And when the joy in our hearts and the light of our minds merge into one, then we are nearing perfection.

I met with the great culture of this prayer on the Holy Mountain, and naturally I wanted to learn of the Fathers – learn how they understood this most important facet of Christian asceticism. I arrived on Mt. Athos in 1925.

[i] John xvi: 24, 23.
[ii] Matt. x: 16.
[iii] Luke x: 17.
[iv] Luke ix: 49.
[v] cf. John xv: 11.

Recently fierce arguments had raged concerning the nature of the Divine Name. The bitter controversy – similar to theological polemics of the 14th century concerning the nature of the Light on Mt. Tabor – had promoted not a few initiatives which ought not to occur among people who have given their souls into the hands of the Almighty. A certain analogy may be drawn in these polemics with the age-old divisions between nominalists and realists, idealists and rationalists. Now they die down, only later to flare up in another guise. Two different natural formations may be observed. On the one side are the prophets and poets. On the other – scientists and technocrats. I do not propose to dwell on the outward aspect of events that occurred at that time, preferring to concentrate on the essence of the problem, in order to apprehend the imperishable knowledge from on High vouchsafed to the holy ascetics, the lovers of mental prayer.

The life of each one of us is linked in the closest fashion with our conceptions of the world, of ourselves and of God. Prayer ultimately demands the most intimate knowledge possible of the real form of Divine Being. 'Beloved, now are we the sons of God [but] it doth not yet appear [in full] what we shall be. We know [by experience] that when he shall appear, we shall be like him; for we shall see him AS HE IS.'[vi] And we also know from the millenary experience of our race that our natural mind left to itself in our given state cannot do more in its reflexions about God than make certain conjectures. It is essential that God Himself manifest Himself to man, giving him knowledge of Him. Just as in the life of each one of us God reveals Himself gradually, so in the history of mankind as shown in the Bible 'at sundry times and in divers manners.'[vii] He revealed Himself to the Fathers and the Prophets with increasing power and depth.

The first mention of the as yet obscure invocation of God

[vi] I John iii: 2.
[vii] Heb. i: 1.

comes in the fourth chapter of Genesis: 'To Seth . . . there was born a son; and he called his name Enos: then began men to call upon the name of the Lord.'[viii] After that God manifested Himself to Abraham, Isaac and Jacob in ever-increasing horizons: 'I appeared unto Abraham, unto Isaac, and unto Jacob, by the name of God Almighty, but by my name JEHOVAH was I not known to them.'[ix] God called Himself the God of Abraham, Isaac and Jacob. But to Moses He 'appeared . . . in a flame of fire . . .' and said, 'I AM THAT I AM'.[x] God completed His revelation of Himself: 'And the Lord descended in the cloud, and stood with him [Moses] there, and proclaimed the name of the LORD. And the LORD passed by before him, and proclaimed, The Lord, The Lord God, merciful and gracious, long-suffering, and abundant in goodness and truth, Keeping mercy [and truth and appearing] for thousands, forgiving iniquity and trans-gression and sin, and that will by no means clear the guilty; visiting the iniquity of the fathers upon the children, and upon the children's children, unto the third and to the fourth generation.'[xi] Thus from the outset God revealed Himself to Moses as PERSONAL and the one true BEING with as yet unknown attributes. Subsequent revelations disclosed the attributes of this I AM as God merciful and lover of mankind. But this, too, was not clear, and Moses admitted to the insufficiency of the knowledge he had acquired.

The prophets likewise did not attain to the fulness they sought; but from the words of Isaiah: 'Thus saith the Lord, your redeemer, the Holy One of Israel . . . I the Lord, the first, and with the last; I am he. Before me there was no God formed, neither shall there be after me.'[xii] This God – 'the First and the Last' – revealed Himself as Personal, as

[viii] Gen. iv: 26.
[ix] Exod. vi: 3.
[x] Exod. iii: 1, 14.
[xi] Exod. xxxiv: 5–7.
[xii] Isa. xliii: 14; xli: 4; xliii: 10.

Living Absolute, not as some abstract 'All-Being' or transpersonal All-One, and the like. (This makes plain that the spirit of the Israeli prophets was concerned with First Being, with Him that is from the Beginning. Such is the attitude characteristic of man, the image of the Absolute. He does not dwell on intermediate matters.) We see in the Bible that every new revelation was perceived as an Epiphany, as God's direct action. Conjunctly, the Very Name Itself was lived as the Presence of God. The Name contained twofold power – a sensation of the Living God for the one part and knowledge of Him for the other. Hence the dread of 'taking His name in vain.'[xiii] With enrichment of revelation of the Divine attributes, of His action, knowledge of God became more profound in general. But despite the Israelites' confidence that they were the chosen people, that the All-Highest revealed Himself to them, until the coming of Christ the groans of the prophets in prayer to God to come on Earth and give total knowledge of Himself – for which the human spirit can never cease hungering – persisted.

God manifested Himself as Providence, Redeemer, Saviour, and much else, but still a veil hung over the human mind. Jacob at the tragic moment of his life after he departed from Laban to return to his father, and where his brother Esau was still living, and whom he dreaded meeting, at night, left alone far from their home ground, fought with God – all those years with Laban had not been easy. He was afraid of Esau's coming. He sought for blessing and protection but in tense conflict he wrestled with Him, accusing Him.[xiv]

A similar contest occurred in the lives of the prophets Elijah and Jonah. Elijah said to the Lord, 'It is enough; now, O Lord, take away my life; for I am not better than my fathers . . . I have been very jealous for the Lord God of hosts: for the children of Israel have forsaken thy covenant, thrown down thine altars, and slain thy prophets with the

[xiii] cf. Exod. xx: 7.
[xiv] Gen. xxxii: 24.

sword; and I, even I only, am left; and they seek my life, to take it away.'[xv.] And Jonah said, 'Lord, Thou didst send me with such force to preach to the Ninevites of the destruction that would come upon them because of their ungodliness though I knew that Thou wouldest not do thus unto them for Thou art a gracious God, and merciful, slow to anger, and of great kindness and repentest thee of evil. Therefore now, O Lord' [that my prophesying was not fulfilled, and I am abashed] 'take my life from me; for it is better for me to die than to live.'[xvi.]

Job is a still more striking instance. 'Let the day perish wherein I was born, and the night in which it was said, There is a man child conceived . . . Let darkness and the shadow of death stain it . . . Let the blackness of the day terrify it. As for that night . . . let it not be joined unto the days of the year; . . . let that night be solitary, let no joyfulness come therein. Let them curse it that curse the day . . . Let it look for the light, but have none; neither let it see the dawning of the day: Because it shut not up the doors of my mother's womb, nor hid sorrow from mine eyes. Why died I not from the womb? why did I not give up the ghost when I came out of the belly? . . . For now should I have lain still and been quiet' [in the great peace of non-being]. 'There the wicked cease from troubling . . . The small and the great are there [in their nothingness]; and the servant is free from his master. Wherefore is light given to him that is in misery, and life unto the bitter in soul; Which long for death, but it cometh not . . . Which rejoice exceedingly, and are glad, when they can find the grave? WHY IS LIGHT GIVEN TO A MAN WHOSE WAY [to knowledge of God] IS HID, AND WHOM GOD HATH HEDGED IN?'[xvii.]

Our lot always contains something in common with each

[xv.] cf. I Kings xix: 4, 10.
[xvi.] Jonah ch. iv.
[xvii.] Job iii.

of them. Israel fought with God and which of us does not so fight. The world even to this day is plunged in despair, nowhere is there any solution. In the wearying struggle the whole earth blames Him for its sufferings. Life is not a simple matter and it is not easy to penetrate the profound purport of Being.

To continue weighed down by the desolation of ignorance is both humiliating and depressing. Our spirit would have direct intercourse with Him, with the One Who called me from nothingness; Who broke up the tranquillity of my non-being and cast me into this absurd — even heinous tragi-comedy. We want to know — with whom lies the iniquity? Is it with us or with Him, the Creator? It seems to us that we came into this world without our wanting to — perhaps even without our consent. Do any of us remember being asked whether we wanted to be born into this life — having been told beforehand what sort of life it would be? Was it open to us to refuse this gift? Are we right when we 'charge God foolishly'?[xviii]

I hear another voice: 'I am the light of the world: he that followeth me shall not walk in darkness, but shall have the light of life.'[xix] 'If any man thirst, let him come unto me, and drink. He that believeth on me . . . out of his belly shall flow rivers of living water.'[xx] Am I not to believe in this appeal on Christ's part, and really fight to attain the Kingdom of the Father's immutable love? To follow the way He, Christ, showed us? If it is not given to us to create anything from 'nothing', then the very idea of eternity cannot be born in us. To have such an idea would be ontologically impossible. If we look carefully at what goes on around us we notice that every real need contains in cosmic being the possibility of being satisfied — one must just find the way. In the history of scientific progress many once seemingly-outrageous

---

[xviii] cf. Job. i: 22.
[xix] John viii: 12.
[xx] John vii: 37, 38.

ideas are now put into effect before our eyes. Why should I doubt that my thirst for blessed immortality and eternal union with the Creator can similarly be realised?

How radically everything alters when the heart suddenly opens to accept Christ's summons! Every moment becomes precious, full of profound meaning. Suffering and joy wondrously merge with new ascetic striving. The ladder to the skies is set up before our eyes.[xxi] 'Thy name shall be called . . . Israel; for hast thou power with God and with man, and hast prevailed.'[xxii] But ask not My Name, for it is wondrous and thou art not yet able to apprehend it. Nevertheless thou art blessed. 'And the sun rose upon him, and he halted upon his thigh.'[xxiii] The way to perfect knowledge was not yet revealed but there was already a glimpse of it. It would deepen in the perception of the prophets, and many fiery words would be said about the Pre-eternal Word of the Father that must come; and the perfect Light, in which there is no darkness at all will be manifest to us in all His might.

To contend with God is fraught with risk. It can lead to perdition but it can also enable us to conquer the 'old man' disfigured by Luciferean pride. Conquer through humility: '. . . and thou shalt overcome men.' How? By humility. 'And Jacob said, O God of my father Abraham and God of my father Isaac . . . Deliver me from the hand of my brother, from the hand of Esau: for I fear him, lest he will come and smite me, and the mother with the children.'[xxiv] . . . 'And Jacob lifted up his eyes, and looked, and, behold, Esau came, and with him four hundred men . . . And he bowed himself to the ground seven times, until he came near to his brother. And Esau ran to meet him, and embraced him, and fell on

[xxi] cf. Gen. xxviii: 12.
[xxii] cf. Gen. xxxii: 28–29.
[xxiii] Gen. xxxii: 31.
[xxiv] Gen. xxxii: 9, 11.

his neck, and kissed him: and they wept.'[xxv.] And Esau was contrite, who had hated Jacob who had cheated him of his father's blessing. In Jacob we have an example of humble repentance.

The present world-wide spiritual crisis – is it not a preparation for a great, fresh renaissance? What is happening now in individual souls can be occurring in a multitude of souls. And it could be like a mighty flood, like a blinding flash of lightning in the midnight dark. The little piece of History allotted to us can and ought to be a period for us in which to assimilate being in all its dimensions. In the light of this hope our very sufferings are like the unwrapping before us of a grandiose picture. 'Day unto day uttereth speech, and night unto night sheweth knowledge'[xxvi.] if they are spent in prayer which goes out 'to the end of the world.' Its [prayer's] going forth is 'from the end of the heaven, and its circuit unto the ends of it: and there is nothing hid from the heat thereof.'[xxvii.] It both warms and rejoices us. It is the channel conveying revelation from on High.

'Blessed be the Name of our God now and for ever.'

The sequence of the revelation of God in the Holy Scriptures tallies to a significant extent with the rhythm of our personal progress. We grow in knowledge like our forefathers and fathers. At first we grasp knowledge of the Highest Being. Then more and more of His attributes become known to the human spirit; and thus the hour approaches of the fearful revelation on Mt. Sinai, 'I AM'.[xxviii.] Following centuries bring more profound knowledge and understanding, though without reaching perfection until the coming of the Awaited One.

He Who is above all Name in His Substance reveals Him-

[xxv.] Gen. xxxiii: 1–4.
[xxvi.] Ps. xix: 2.
[xxvii.] Ps. xix: 6.
[xxviii.] Exod. iii: 14.

self to the reasonable beings created in His image under many names: Eternal, All-knowing, Almighty; Light, Life, Beauty, Wisdom; Goodness, Truth, Love; Saviour, Hallowed, *et al.* In each and through all of these we feel the presence of the One God, and in virtue of His indivisibility we possess Him altogether. It is meet to think thus but at the same time not one of these attributes affords us full comprehension of Him 'as He is'. His Being in Its Essence transcends all Names. And yet He goes on revealing Himself in Names.

Twenty centuries ago, according to our reckoning, He came, He Whom the peoples awaited, the Logos of the Father. Above the world in His Essence, the Creator of our nature 'took upon him the form of a servant, and was made in the likeness of man.'[xxix] The Unoriginate Word of the Father 'was made flesh, and dwelt among us.'[xxx] The Eternal manifested Himself in time. The revelation brought us a new Name: JESUS, Saviour, or GOD-the-SAVIOUR. A great Light came into the life of the world. A new epoch began. History from Adam to Moses was holy. It was holy from the moment of the Appearance of God on Mt. Sinai; and holier still from the moment of the coming of Christ.

The idea of God the Saviour existed even earlier but with a different connotation, in another dimension, incomparably less concrete. 'The people which sat in darkness saw great light; and to them which sat in the region and shadow of death light is sprung up.'[xxxi]

The Name Jesus first and foremost indicates to us the purpose of God's coming in the flesh 'for our salvation'. In assuming our nature God indicates the possibility for us, too, to become sons of God. Our sonship lies in the communication to us of the divine form of being: 'For in him dwelleth all the fulness of the Godhead bodily.'[xxxii] At the Ascension

[xxix] cf. Phil. ii: 7.
[xxx] John i: 14.
[xxxi] Matt. iv: 16.
[xxxii] Col. ii: 9.

He sat at the right hand of the Father and as the Son of Man. This is how He tells it Himself: 'The glory which thou gavest me I have given them; that they may be one, even as we are one: I in them, and thou in me, that they may be made perfect in one; and that the world may know that thou hast sent me, and hast loved them, as thou hast loved me. Father, I will that they also, whom thou hast given me, be with me where I am; that they may behold my glory, which thou hast given me: for thou lovedst me before the foundation of the world . . . And I have declared unto them thy name, and will declare it: that the love wherewith thou hast loved me may be in them, and I in them.'[xxxiii]

Our mind falls silent in wonder before this mystery – the Creator took upon Himself our created flesh. The Eternal and Invisible assumed a temporal and mutable form of being. The Spirit, beyond all our thinking, became flesh and let us touch Him with our hands, look on Him with our physical eyes. The passionless One gave Himself over to suffering. The Unoriginate Life tied Himself to death.

The philosophising mind confronted with itself cannot come to terms with the Gospel preaching. It seems crazy. The Absolute of the philosophers in their works was not permitted to 'take upon Him the form of a servant, and be made in the likeness of men.'[xxxiv] According to them the Absolute in essence is non-being (in the full sense of the word). Before the coming of Christ there were minds who invented for themselves very attractive theories about this sort of abstract Absolute. And for us in our day the appearance of such tendencies is nothing new. Unfortunately, many fall victim to this spiritual aberration. St. Paul penned a brilliant canticle on the subject: 'For it is written, I will destroy the wisdom of the wise, and will bring to nothing the understanding of the prudent . . . For it pleased God by the foolishness of preaching to save them that believe. For

[xxxiii] John xvii: 22–26.
[xxxiv] cf. Phil. ii: 7.

131

the Jews require a sign, and the Greeks seek after wisdom: But we preach Christ crucified, unto the Jews a stumbling-block, and unto the Greeks foolishness; But unto them which are called . . . Christ the power of God, and the wisdom of God. Because the foolishness of God is wiser than men; and the weakness of God is stronger than men.'[xxxv.]

'The Word was made flesh, and dwelt among us.'[xxxvi.] We are unable to apprehend how this is possible but we do not rule out that He Who created our nature could assume it into His own Hypostasis. He did not assume a new, different hypostasis, a human hypostasis. Continuing in His eternal Hypostasis as God, He conjoined in It divine nature with created nature. In the flesh He manifested the Father's perfection to us – with extraordinary force He demonstrated the conjunction of God and Man.

Christ brought us knowledge of the Holy Trinity: of the Father and the Son and the Holy Spirit. Moses understood GOD – I AM – as One Person. The Word and the Spirit were for him the energy of One Being. And we know that both the Logos and the Spirit are Hypostases equal with the Father: One in Substance, plural in Persons. The image of this God is a single human nature in a multiple of hypostases.

By virtue of the unity of God the name I AM applies likewise to all the Trinity and to each Hypostasis separately. Like many other Names, this Name can and must be understood both as a common appellative and as proper to each Person – in the same way as the Name 'Lord' refers likewise to all Three Persons and at the same time serves as the proper Name for each of the Three. The same can be said about the Name JESUS – that is, God the Saviour. But in our practice of prayer we use this Name JESUS exclusively as Christ's own Name, the Second Person of the Holy Trinity.

In ancient times the human spirit gained knowledge of the Divinity through Names which spoke mainly of the

[xxxv.] I Cor. i: 19–25.
[xxxvi.] John i: 14.

Divine attributes – power, omnipresence, omniscience, providence, glory and so on. To Moses God said that His Name was I AM. Through the incarnation of the Logos of the Father we come into contact with God in such a form, such fulness, that we look no further, needing only to live an ascetic life according to the commandments in order to apprehend the gift in its true dimensions: He lived with us, in the conditions of our fall. He spoke to us in our tongue. He came down to us to such a degree that we could touch Him. In visible form He showed us the Invisible Father to perfection. He made known to us all that concerns relations between God and man. The salvation He brought is exceptionally concrete. He started His preaching with the summons: 'Repent: for the kingdom of heaven is at hand.'[xxxvii] In this homily we see the sequel to His discourse with Adam in paradise.[xxxviii]

Great is the Name I AM. Great the Name of the Holy Trinity. And great, too, the name JESUS. Much can be said of this Name of His. It is inexhaustible in its content. It belongs to Him to Whom everything that is owes its existence. 'All things were made by him; and without him was not any thing made that was made. In him was life; and the life was the light of men.'[xxxix] He was 'in the beginning' – that is, He is the principle of all the universe. In the inner life of the Trinity He is turned towards the Father; in the Act of creation that Logos addressed Himself to the creature in His image.

The Name Jesus as knowledge, as 'energy' of God in relation to the world and as His proper Name, is ontologically bound up with Him. It is spiritual reality. Its sound can merge with its reality but not necessarily so. As a name it was given to many mortal men but when we pray we utter

[xxxvii] Matt. iv: 17.
[xxxviii] cf. Gen. iii: 8 et seq.
[xxxix] John i: 3, 4.

it with another content, another 'frame' of spirit. For us it is the bridge between us and Him. It is the canal along which the streams of divine strength flow to us. As proceeding from the Holy God it is holy and it hallows us by its invocation. With this Name and through it prayer acquires a certain tangibleness: it unites us with God. In it, this Name, God is present like a scent-flask full of fragrance. Through it, the Celestial One can be sensed imminently. As divine energy it proceeds from the Substance of Divinity and is divine itself.

When we pray, knowing this, our prayer becomes at the same time both a fearful and a triumphal act. In ancient times the commandment bade us not to take the Name of God in vain. The Lord gave the commandment and bidding to 'ask of the Father in His Name'. Through the coming of Christ all the Divine Names were disclosed to us in their more profound sense, and we ought to stand in fear and trembling, as happens with many ascetics among whom I came to live, when they pronounce the Holy Name of Jesus. It is bold of me to say that even I could have been a living witness that fitting invocation of this Name fills all our being with the presence of the Eternal God; carries our mind into other Spheres; endows us with the peculiar energy of a new life. Divine Light, which it is not easy to discuss, comes with this Name.

We know that not only the Name Jesus but all the other Names, too, are revealed to us from on High, are ontologically linked with Him – God. We know this from experience in the Church. All the sacraments in our Church are effected by invocation of the Divine Names, first and foremost of the Holy Trinity: of the Father and of the Son and of the Holy Spirit. All our divine worship is based on invocation of the Divine Names. We do not attribute magic powers to them, as sound phenomena. They are pronounced in true confession of our faith and in a state of divine awe, reverence and love – we do indeed hold God conjointly with His Names. Many generations of the priesthood have preserved knowledge of the power of the Name of God and performed the sacraments with a profound sense of the presence of the Living God. The sacrament of the celebration of the Divine Liturgy was revealed to them. For them there was no doubt that the Blood and the Body of Christ lay before them in all their reality. Over the bread and the wine the Name was invoked of Him Who, when He pronounces the word, the word becomes 'fact'. 'And God said, Let there be light: and there was light.'[xl.]

Neglect of the ontological character of the Divine Names, the lack of this experience in prayers and the celebration of the divine office has desolated the lives of many. For them prayer and the sacraments themselves lose their eternal reality. The Liturgy becomes, not a Divine Act but simply a psychological or mental commemoration. Many go so far as to think prayer a useless waste of time, especially if their prayer for our everyday needs does not bring about what they prayed for . . . But is not the union with the God of our being the most important miracle of our existence? The 'good part' which death shall not take from us.[xli.] The fact of our resurrection in God – this is what our attention is centred on as the final purport of our appearance in the world. Love for Christ, filling the whole man, radically alters our life. He – God-man – united the two in Himself, and through Him we have access to the Father. Could one wish for anything more?

Those who have come to love Christ and His Name delight in reading the Gospels and the Holy Scriptures generally. The Divine Names, the Purport and Light proceeding from them, draw the spirit of man to themselves and naught else can captivate him. With what heavenly inspiration St. Peter says, 'There is none other name under heaven given among

---

[xl.] Gen. i: 3.
[xli.] cf. Luke x: 42.

men, whereby we must be saved.'[xlii] Or, 'Silver and gold have I none; but such as I have give I thee: In the name of Jesus Christ of Nazareth rise up and walk.'[xliii] On another occasion the Apostles lifted up their voices to God and said: 'Lord, thou art God, which hast made heaven, and earth, and all that in them is . . . Behold their threatenings [of the kings and sovereigns of this world – the Herods and Pilates, the Gentiles, and the people of Israel] and grant unto thy servants, that with all boldness they may speak thy word, by stretching forth thine hand to heal; and that signs and wonders may be done by the name of thy holy child Jesus.'[xliv]

And so all the Holy Scriptures from beginning to end witness to God through His Name. And our spirit never ceases to delight in the sacred words, and the soul blesses God Who gave us this priceless gift.

Man develops slowly in the sphere of knowledge of God. Years and years elapse before we can appreciate the grand scenario that is Genesis: the creation of the world with its cosmic forces and phenomena, and Man when 'the Lord God . . . breathed into his nostrils the breath of life.'[xlv] Man is the principle linking God and the rest of creation since he is the principle conjoining created cosmic energies with the Uncreated. Every energy proceeding from God, from Divine Being, theologians term 'divine'. Substance, however, is not communicable to man but Divine life is conjoined with man by the power of Divine action. The act of divinisation is effected through uncreated grace. The transfiguration on Mt. Tabor is the most striking instance of this in the New Testament: in the Light seen by the Apostles they heard the voice of the Father saying, 'This is my beloved Son.'[xlvi] Both the Light and the Voice (both inexplicable) were 'divine'.

[xlii] Acts iv: 12.
[xliii] Acts iii: 6.
[xliv] Acts iv: 24–33.
[xlv] Gen. ii: 7.
[xlvi] Matt. xvii: 5.

It is essential for all of us to learn to distinguish energies according to their source. Inability to do this slows up the process of our growth in the spirit.

It is not out of place here to point out that there is nothing automatic or magical about the Jesus Prayer. If we do not strive to obey His commandments, calling upon His Name will be in vain. He Himself said, 'Many will say to me in that day, Lord, Lord, have we not prophesied in thy name? and in thy name have cast out devils? and in thy name done many wonderful works? And then will I profess unto them, I never knew you: depart from me, ye that work iniquity.'[xlvii] It is very important that we should become like Moses who 'endured, as seeing him who is invisible,'[xlviii] and invoke Him recognising the ontological connection between the Name and Him Who is named, with the Person of Christ. Love for Him will grow and perfect itself in proportion as our cognition of the life of the beloved God increases and deepens. When we are fond of a fellow human being, it is pleasant to pronounce his name which we do not grow tired of repeating. Thus it is, and immeasurably more so, with the Name of the Lord. When someone we love further and further reveals his talents, then we value him more and more and take pleasure in noting new features in him. Thus is it with the Name of Jesus Christ. With gripping interest we discover new mysteries in His Name of the ways of God, and ourselves become bearers of the reality contained in the Name. Through this organic cognition in the very experience of our life we become partakers of eternity. 'This is life eternal, that they might know thee the only true God, and Jesus Christ, whom thou hast sent.'[xlix]

'O Lord Jesus Christ, Son of God, have mercy on us and on thy world.'

[xlvii] Matt. vii: 22–23.
[xlviii] Heb. xi: 27.
[xlix] John xvii: 3.

The name Jesus was given to us by a revelation from on High. It proceeds from the eternal Divine sphere and is in no way the product of any earthly mind although it is expressed by an everyday human word. Revelation is an act – the energy of Divinity, and as such belongs on another plane, and transcends cosmic energies. In its celestial glory the Name Jesus is meta-cosmic. When we pronounce the Name of Christ, calling upon Him to communion with us, then He, all-fulfilling, hears us, and we enter into living contact with Him. As the pre-eternal Logos of the Father He dwells in undivided unity with Him, and God-the-Father through His Word enters into communion with us. Christ is the Only-begotten, co-eternal Son of the Father, and therefore says, 'No man cometh unto the Father, but by me.'[l.] The Name Jesus means God-the-Saviour; as such it can be applied to the Holy Trinity. It is applicable to each Hypostasis separately. But in our prayer we use the Name Jesus exclusively as the proper Name of the God-Man, and our attention is turned to Him. 'In him dwelleth all the fulness of the Godhead bodily,'[li.] says St. Paul. In Him there is not only God but all the human race also. Praying the Name of Jesus Christ, we place ourselves before the absolute fulness of both the Uncreated First-Being and created being. To enter into the realm of this fulness of Being we must install Him in us so that His life becomes ours through invocation of His Name, according to the commandment: Lord, Jesus Christ, Son of God, have mercy on me, a sinner. 'He that is joined unto the Lord is one spirit.'[lii.]

I have dwelt on the dogmatic interpretation of the JESUS PRAYER to a considerable extent because in the last decade I have often come across perverted ideas about the practice of this Prayer. The most inacceptable are those identifying it

[l.] John xiv: 6.
[li.] Col. ii: 9.
[lii.] I Cor. vi: 17.

with yoga, Buddhism and even 'transcendental meditation,' and the like. The radical distinction between all these deviations from Christianity consists in the fact that at the root of our life is the Revelation of a PERSONAL God: I AM. All other paths deflect our mind from the personal interrelationship between God and the one who prays into the realm of abstract trans-personal Absolute, into impersonal asceticism.

In diverting our mind from all images, meditation can afford us a sense of tranquility, of peace, a release from time and space, but there is no feeling of standing before a personal God. It is not real prayer — face to Face. This can lead to a state where one who is entranced by meditation will be content with the psychical results of such experiments and, worst of all, perception of the Living God, the Personal Absolute, will be alien to him. Not seldom do we see senseless attempts over a short period to attain 'cosmic knowledge' and even direct contact with the Supra-Personal Absolute. Actually, this kind of asceticism constitutes departure from the True God, from Him Who in truth is.

Gospel teaching speaks not only of a Personal God but of the individual immortality of those being redeemed. This is achieved through victory over the world of the passions. A noble, a grandiose task; but the Lord said, 'Be of good cheer; I have overcome the world;'[liii.] and we know that this was not an easy victory. Again Christ teaches: 'Enter ye in at the strait gate: for wide is the gate, and broad is the way, that leadeth to destruction, and many there be which go in thereat: Because strait is the gate, and narrow is the way, which leadeth unto life, and few there be that find it. Beware of false prophets . . .'[liv.] Wherein lies perdition? In that people forsake the Living God revealed to us, to concentrate on that 'nothing' from which they were called into being for immor-

[liii.] John xvi: 33.
[liv.] Matt. vii: 13–15.

139

tal blessedness in the form of sonship of God, through the establishment in them of God the Holy Trinity.

To believe in Christ, either childlike simplicity is needed – 'Except ye be converted, and become as little children, ye shall not enter into the kingdom of heaven'[lv.] – or to become like Paul who in mindless audacity said, 'We are fools for Christ's sake . . . we are weak . . . we are despised . . . we are made as the filth of the world, and are the offscouring of all things unto this day.'[lvi.] And yet, 'For other foundation can no man lay than that is laid, which is Jesus Christ.'[lvii.] 'I beseech you, be ye followers of me, as I of Christ.'[lviii.]

Cosmic knowledge in the Christian experience is given in prayer like the Lord's Gesthsemane prayer, and not in philosophic transcension. 'And he said unto them . . . thus it behoved . . . that repentance and remission of sins should be preached IN HIS NAME among all nations . . . And ye are witnesses of these things. And, behold, I send the promise of my Father upon you: but tarry ye [in prayer] until ye be endued with power from on high.'[lix.]

[lv.] Matt. xviii: 3.
[lvi.] I Cor. iv: 10–13.
[lvii.] I Cor. iii: 11.
[lviii.] cf. I Cor. iv: 16; xi: 1.
[lix.] cf. Luke xxiv: 46–49.

II

The JESUS PRAYER
Method

I propose to devote this chapter to setting out as briefly as possible the more important aspects of the Jesus Prayer and the common-sense views regarding this great culture of the heart that I met with on the Holy Mountain.

Year after year monks repeat this prayer with their lips, without trying by any artificial means to join mind and heart. Their attention is concentrated on harmonising their everyday life with the commandments of Christ. According to ancient tradition mind unites with heart through Divine action when the monk continues in the ascetic feat of obedience and abstinence; when the mind, the heart and the very body of the 'old man' to a sufficient degree are freed from the dominion over them of sin. However, both early and present-day teachers occasionally permit recourse to a technical method of bringing the mind down into the heart. To do this the monk, having suitably settled his body, pronounces the prayer with his head inclined on his chest, breathing in at the words, 'Lord, Jesus Christ, (Son of God)' and breathing out to the words, 'Have mercy upon me (a sinner).' During inhalation the attention at first follows the movement of the air breathed in as far as the upper part of the heart. In this manner concentration can soon be preserved without wandering, and the mind stands side by side with the heart, or even enters within it. This method eventually enables the mind to see, not the physical heart but that which is happening within it – the feelings that

141

creep in and the mental images that approach from without. With this experience the monk acquires the ability to feel his heart, and to continue with his attention centred in the heart without further recourse to any psychosomatic technique.

This procedure can assist the beginner to understand where his inner attention should be stayed during prayer and, as a rule, at all other times, too. Nevertheless, true prayer is not to be achieved thus. True prayer comes exclusively through faith and repentance accepted as the only foundation. The danger of psychotechnics is that not a few of us attribute too great significance to method *qua* method. In order to avoid such deformation the beginner should follow another practice which, though considerably slower is incomparably better and more wholesome – to fix the attention on the Name of Jesus Christ and on the words of the prayer. When contrition for sin reaches a certain level the mind naturally heeds the heart.

The complete formula of the Jesus Prayer runs like this: *Lord Jesus Christ, Son of God, have mercy upon me, a sinner*, and it is this set form that is recommended to the beginner. In the first half of the prayer we profess Christ-God made flesh for our salvation. In the second we affirm our fallen state, our sinfulness and our redemption. The conjunction of dogmatic confession with repentance makes the content of the prayer more comprehensive.

It is possible to establish a certain sequence in the development of this prayer. First, it is a verbal matter: we say the prayer with our lips while trying to concentrate our attention on the Name and the words. Next, we no longer move our lips but pronounce the Name of Jesus Christ, and what follows after, in our minds, mentally. In the third stage mind and heart combine to act together: the attention of the mind is centred in the heart and the prayer is said there. Fourthly, the prayer becomes self-propelling. This happens when the prayer is confirmed in the heart and, with no especial effort on our part, continues there, where the mind is concentrated. Finally, the prayer, so full of blessing, starts to act like a gentle flame within us, as inspiration from on High, rejoicing the heart with a sensation of Divine love and delighting the mind in spiritual contemplation. This last state is sometimes accompanied by a vision of Light.

A gradual ascent into prayer is the most trustworthy. The beginner who would embark on the struggle is usually recommended to start with the first step, verbal prayer, until body, tongue, brain and heart assimilate it. The time this takes varies. The more earnest the repentance, the shorter the road.

The practice of mental prayer may for a while be associated with the hesychastic method – in other words, it may take the form of rhythmic or a-rhythmic articulation of the prayer as described above, by breathing in during the first half and breathing out during the second part. This can be genuinely helpful if one does not lose sight of the fact that every invocation of the Name of Christ must be inseparably coupled with a consciousness of Christ Himself. The Name must not be detached from the Person of God, lest prayer be reduced to a technical exercise and so contravene the commandment, 'Thou shalt not take the name of the Lord thy God in vain.'[i]

When the attention of the mind is fixed in the heart it is possible to control what happens in the heart, and the battle against the passions assumes a rational character. The enemy is recognised and can be driven off by the power of the Name of Christ. With this ascetic feat the heart becomes so highly sensitive, so discerning, that eventually when praying for anyone the heart can tell almost at once the state of the person being prayed for. Thus the transition takes place from mental prayer to prayer of the mind-and-heart, which may be followed by the gift of prayer that proceeds of itself.

We try to stand before God with the whole of our being.

[i] Exod. xx: 7; Deut. v: 11.

143

Invocation of the Name of God the Saviour, uttered in the fear of God, together with a constant effort to live in accordance with the commandments, little by little leads to a blessed fusion of all our powers, disintegrated by the Fall. We must never seek to hurry in our ascetic striving. It is essential to discard the idea of achieving the maximum in the shortest possible time. God does not force us but neither can we compel Him to anything whatsoever. Results obtained by artificial means do not last long and, more importantly, do not unite our spirit with the Spirit of the Living God.

In the atmosphere of the world today prayer requires super-human courage. The whole ensemble of cosmic energies waits in opposition. To hold on to prayer without distraction signals victory on every level of natural existence. The way is long and thorny but there comes a moment when a ray of Divine Light pierces the thick gloom, to make an opening through which we can glimpse the Source of this Light. The Jesus Prayer then assumes cosmic and meta-cosmic dimensions.

'Exercise thyself rather unto godliness. For bodily exercise profiteth little: but godliness is profitable unto all things, having promise of the life that now is, and of that which is to come. This is a faithful saying and worthy of all acceptation. For therefore we labour . . . because we trust in the living God, who is the Saviour of all men . . . These things command and teach.'[ii] Following this teaching of the Apostle will be the surest route to Him Whom we seek. I am not thinking here of artificial means of achieving divinisation — we believe that God came down on earth and revealed to us the secret of sin, and gave us the grace of repentance, and we pray, 'O Lord Jesus Christ, Son of God, have mercy upon me, a sinner,' in the hope of forgiveness and reconciliation in His Name. We never, to the end of our lives let go of the words, 'Forgive me, a sinner.' Total victory over sin is only possible if God Himself comes to live in us, which will be

[ii] I Tim. iv: 7–11.

our divinisation, too, making possible direct contemplation of God 'as He is.' Fulness of Christian perfection is not to be attained within the bounds of this Earth. St. John the Divine writes, 'No man hath seen God at any time; the only begotten Son, which is in the bosom of the Father, he hath declared him.'[iii] And it is St. John who asserts that in the time to come our divinisation will be complete 'for we shall see him AS HE IS. And every man that hath this hope in him purifieth himself, even as He is pure ... Whosoever abideth in him sinneth not: whosoever sinneth hath not seen him, neither known him.'[iv] It is salutary to take in the contents of this Epistle, so that invoking the Name of Jesus may become effective, a means of salvation; that we may 'pass from death unto life;'[v] that we may be 'endued with power from on high.'[vi]

One of the most remarkable books, works of the ascetic fathers, is the 'Ladder' of St. John Climacus. Newly-professed monks read it, and it also serves as an authoritative criterion for the 'perfect'. (No need, perhaps, to point out that perfection on this earth is never complete.) The same can be said of the Jesus Prayer. Simple pious folk, whatever the work they are engaged in pray it. It takes the place of church services. Monks pronounce it mentally during the offices in church. And it is their primary occupation in their cells, as for hesychasts in the desert.

Repetition of the Jesus Prayer is bound up in the closest fashion with the theology of the Divine Name. It has profound dogmatic roots, just as dogmatic consciousness harmoniously accompanies all forms of ascetic life. Indeed, in some of its forms it becomes 'a consuming fire.'[vii] It contains

[iii] John i: 18.
[iv] I John iii: 2, 3, 6.
[v] cf. I John iii: 14.
[vi] Luke xxiv: 49.
[vii] Heb. xii: 29.

divine strength restoring the dead from their sins; light enlightening the mind, communicating the capacity to see the powers acting in the 'cosmos'. And it affords us the possibility of contemplating what goes on in our heart and mind. 'It pierces even to the dividing asunder of soul and spirit, and of the joints and marrow, and is a discerner of the thoughts and intents of the heart.'[viii.]

Reverent praying of this prayer brings one up against many contrary energies concealed in the atmosphere. Offered in a state of deep repentance, the prayer penetrates into the realm beyond the bounds of the 'wisdom of the wise and the understanding of the prudent.'[ix.] In its more intense manifestations it demands either much experience or a mentor. Vigilant caution, a contrite spirit and fear of God, and patience with all that befalls us are essential for everyone without exception. Then the prayer becomes a force uniting our spirit with the Divine Spirit, affording us a feeling of the living presence within us of eternity, first having led us through the black darkness hidden within us.

This prayer is a great gift of Heaven to man and mankind.

The importance of continuing in − not to say, practising − the Jesus Prayer the experience itself shows.

Understanding the 'mechanics' of mental prayer is easy for a contemporary educated man. He just has to pray for two or three weeks with a certain diligence, read some books and lo, he can add his own to the existing number. But at the hour of death, when our whole structure undergoes a violent break-up; when the brain loses its lucidity and the heart experiences either fierce pain or enfeeblement − then all our theoretical knowledge goes by the board, and prayer can vanish.

It is essential to continue with praying for years on end; to read little and then only what touches upon prayer and by its content urges us to repentant prayer in the inner

[viii.] cf. Heb. iv: 12.
[ix.] cf. I Cor. i: 19.

confines of the mind. Long-continuing prayer becomes part of our nature, our natural reaction to every occurrence in the spiritual sphere, be it light or darkness; the appearance of holy angels or demonic powers; be it joy or sorrow – in a word, all the time, in all circumstances.

With such prayer our birth into the world can indeed be 'without pain'.

The New Testament is a short book, opening to us the last depths of unoriginate Being. The theory of the Jesus Prayer likewise does not need to go to lengths. The perfection shewn to us by Christ is unattainable within earthly bounds. It is impossible to describe the multitudinous ordeals suffered by the striver for this prayer. Practising this prayer in a strange fashion leads man's spirit to encounter the 'forces' hidden in the Cosmos. It, this prayer, the Jesus Prayer, arouses conflict with the cosmic powers, 'against the rulers of the darkness of this world, against spiritual wickedness in high places.'[x] Lifting one into the sphere lying beyond the bounds of earthly wisdom, in its loftiest forms it does indeed require 'an angel, faithful guide'.

The Jesus Prayer in essence ranks superior to any other outward form but in practice, because of our inability to continue in it for a long time 'with a pure mind', the faithful make use of a chaplet. On the Holy Mountain the most commonly-used chaplet had a hundred knots divided into four sections (each having twenty-five knots). The number of prayers and prostrations per day and night depends on the strength of the individual monk and the general time-table of his Monastery.

[x] Ephesians vi: 12.

III

The JESUS PRAYER for all times and occasions

Whoever really believes that the Gospel commandments were given by the One True God, from this very belief draws strength to live in the image of Christ. The believer allows no critical approach to the Lord's word but looks to it for judgment. Like this he recognises himself as a sinner and grieves over his wretched state. Absence of grief for one's sin indicates that one has not yet been granted the vision of how man was conceived before the creation of the world. The truly repentant sinner does not seek after sublime contemplation: he is totally preoccupied with the battle against sin, against the passions. Only after being cleansed from the passions – still as yet incompletely – naturally and without constraint do hitherto unsuspected spiritual horizons, illumined by light, open before him, and mind and heart are raptured by divine love. Then is our nature re-formed, which was fractured by the Fall, and the doors to the realm of immortality are set ajar.

The way to holy contemplation is through repentance. So long as we are possessed by sombre pride out of character with God – the Light in which 'is no darkness at all'[i.] – we are not accepted into His eternity. But this passion is peculiarly subtle, and we ourselves have not the power to discern its presence in us fully. Hence our assiduous prayer, 'Cleanse thou me from secret faults. Keep back thy servant also from presumptuous sins; let them not have dominion over me: then shall I be upright, and I shall be innocent from the great

---

[i.] cf. I John i: 5.

transgression. Let the words of my mouth, and the meditation of my heart, be acceptable in thy sight, O Lord, my strength, and my redeemer.'[ii]

None of us, sons of Adam, clearly perceive our sins. Only at times of enlightenment by Divine Light are we freed from these dreadful fetters. And if this does not come about, it is well to cry out with tears:[iii]

O Lord Jesus Christ, Son of God, have mercy upon me, a sinner.

Earnest obedience to Christ's commandments involves encountering every possible phenomenon of the spiritual cosmic sphere. By himself man is incapable of either resisting or clearly discerning what destroys and what redeems. In despair he will call upon the Name of the Living God. And blessed will he be if a ray of Light shines upon him from the unapproachable realm of Divinity which will reveal the true nature of every phenomenon. But if this Light has not come yet, he must not be alarmed but pray vigorously, 'O Lord Jesus Christ, Son of the Living God, have mercy upon me,' and saving strength will surely descend on him.

At the outset of our ascetic struggle we do not discern the ways directed to us by God. We try to avoid the painful effort, the 'fiery trial.'[iv] We can continue in an excruciating state of not understanding why God, all-perfect love, at times allows the way to Him to become fearful. We beseech Him to open to us the mystery of the path to salvation. Gradually our mind is enlightened, and our heart gathers strength to follow Christ and through our insignificant sufferings join Him in His sufferings. It is imperative that we should experience both pain and horror, if the depths of being are to be disclosed to us, and for us to become capable of the love commanded of us. In the absence of suffering man remains

---

[ii] Ps. xix: 12–14.
[iii] cf. Heb. v: 7; Job xvi: 20.
[iv] I Pet. iv: 12.

spiritually lazy, half asleep, devoid of Christ. Aware of this, when our heart becomes like an extinct volcano we warm it up by invoking the Name of Christ:

'O Lord Jesus Christ, Son of the Living God, have mercy upon me.'

And the flame of Divine love will indeed touch upon the heart.

Succeeding in the Jesus Prayer means attaining eternal life. In the very grave moments of the break-up of our physical organism the prayer 'O Jesus Christ' clothes our soul. When our brain stops functioning and all other prayers become difficult to remember and pronounce, the light of knowledge of God proceeding from the Name which we know intimately will continue imprescriptible in our spirit. Having witnessed the death of my fathers, who died in prayer, I have a strong hope that heavenly peace, 'which passeth all understanding'[v.] will embrace us for ever. 'O Jesus, save me . . . O Jesus Christ, have mercy, save me . . . O Jesus, save me . . . O Jesus, my God.'

The triumph – the gentle, holy triumph – of knowing the God of love rouses in our souls profound compassion for all mankind. This all-man is my nature, my body, my life and love. I cannot divest myself of my 'nature', detach myself from my 'body', one cell continually torn off from another though they all constitute one organism. This great 'all-man' body continually exists in a state of painful break-up of its parts which are not under our control. The affliction is incurable. And this is our destiny on the earthly plane. The soul weeps in prayer to the point of exhaustion but salvation only comes if people themselves of their own free will desire it. 'Love your enemies' – herein lies both the healing of life on this earth and salvation for eternity. He who has learned the power of love for one's enemies now knows the Lord Jesus, crucified for His enemies. He has anticipated his own

[v.] Phil. iv: 7.

resurrection also, and the Kingdom of Christ, who hath overcome the world.[vi.]

'O Almighty Lord, Christ Jesus, have mercy upon us and upon Thy world.'

In the world of man's spiritual being Christianity provides the experience of the uncreated Light of Divinity and the outer darkness of hell. Such fulness of knowledge is only to be attained through Christ-God and the Holy Spirit. We see in the history of the ascetic striving of our Fathers that it was given to them existentially to contemplate the darkness of hell. And this to such an extent that people of exceptional courage year after year groaned and wept in their prayers. But who can talk about such matters? The mystery is hid from those lacking actual living experience, until the time comes for the Last Judgment.[vii.]

'Lord Jesus Christ, save us.'

It is a great gift to contemplate eternity in the unapproachable Light of Divinity. No one who has experienced this bliss will strive after transitory treasures. This grace does not continue with man for ever and the Light fades in his soul. Being bereft of *such* a God provokes suffering in our whole being – but such deprivation is essential for each and all lest one should rest on one's laurels instead of continuing to follow after the Lord to Golgotha, the highest of all mountains on the plane of the Spirit. However feeble the effort it does all the same regenerate man, giving him new strength to take on likeness to Christ.

'O Lord, our Saviour, save me, a sinner.'

When we pray in a quiet solitary place quite often useless thoughts persistently gather about the mind, distracting attention from the heart. Prayer seems futile because the

[vi.] John xvii: 21–23; xi: 51–52; Eph. ii: 14–17; I Cor. iii: 22; *et al.*
[vii.] cf. Matt. xxv: 31 *et seq.*

mind is not taking part in the invocation of the Name of Jesus – only the lips mechanically repeat the words. And when the prayer comes to an end, extraneous thoughts then generally go away, leaving one in peace. However, there is some sense in this tedious business: in invoking the Divine Name we set in motion all that is concealed in us. Prayer is like shafts of light cast on the dark depths of our inner life, showing us what passions or attachments are lodged in us. When this happens we must urgently pronounce the Holy Name, so that a feeling of repentance increases in the soul.

'O Lord Jesus Christ, Son of God, have mercy upon me, a sinner.'

Our spirit, imperishable according to God's design for us, wearies in the prison-cell of sinful passions. The more acute our distress over our distance from God because of sin, the fiercer our soul's upsurge towards Him; and the soul prays in anguish, sheds many tears, seeking to be united to Him. And He does not despise the repentant heart, and comes to us; and the 'deep' heart of man realises its kinship with Him 'perceptibly' present and active within us. From this it is evident that our body, too, reacts characteristically and breathes the breath of the Living God:

'O Jesus, Son of the Living God, have mercy upon us.'

Our legacy inherited from the Fathers – their teaching and accounts of God's gifts – also indicates the ways to knowledge of God, of the battle in our inner selves against the 'law of sin'[viii.] in each one of us, that tragic consequence of the first fall of man. Everyone who has embarked on the complex struggle for godly eternity will meet, *inter alia*, with the necessity to resist the influence of the world around us, thrusting us against prayer. Again, our best defence is prayer:

'O Lord Jesus Christ, have mercy upon us and Thy world.'

[viii.] cf. Rom. vii: 23.

The Name of Jesus Christ for the believer is like a high fortress-wall. It is not easy for the enemy to cheat his way through the heavy iron gates if our attention is not distracted by outside concerns. The Jesus Prayer gives the soul the strength to resist harmful influences from outside. It does even more. It affords us the possibility to influence the *milieu* in which we live – to emerge, as it were, from the inner depths of our mind and heart and mix with our brethren in love and peace. Increasing peace and love, commanded by God, induce ardent prayer for the whole world. The spirit of Christ draws us into expanses of love embracing all creation, so that the soul prays urgently:

'O Lord Jesus Christ, our Saviour, have mercy upon us and upon Thy world.'

God never coerces. Nor can anyone constrain Him either. In our prayer we try to stand as a whole, uniting all our being, heart and mind most of all. In order to achieve this blessed union of the two most important components of our personality we do not have recourse to any artificial means (psychotechnics). To begin with we train the mind to continue attentive in prayer, as the Fathers teach – that is, carefully pronounce the Divine Name of Jesus Christ and the rest of the prayer. Concentrated invocation of the Divine Name together with unremitting effort to live one's life in accordance with the Gospel commandments leads to a state where both mind and heart actually function together.

We must never try to make haste in our ascetic striving. It is essential to dismiss the idea of achieving the maximum result in the shortest time. Experience down the centuries shows that fusion of mind and heart achieved psychotechnically never lasts long; and, more importantly, does not unite our spirit with the Spirit of the Living God. Eternal salvation in the most profound sense is the question that lies before us. For this our whole nature must be reborn, the carnal to become spiritual. And when the Lord finds us able to take in His grace He is not slow to respond to our humble invocations. His coming is sometimes so all-consuming that heart and mind are both completely occupied by Him only. This visible world gives place to a reality of another, higher order. The mind ceases to think discursively: it becomes all attention. And the heart finds itself in a state difficult to describe: it is filled with fear but a reverent, life-giving fear. Breathing is restrained: God is seen both within and without. He fills all things, all of man: mind-spirit, heart-feeling and even the body, all together, live only through God.

'O Lord Jesus Christ, our God, have mercy upon us and upon Thy world.'

I have ventured to speak of things that a monk usually keeps a precious secret within himself, for fear lest 'Jesus convey himself away.'[ix] It was given me to learn of this while I was still living in the Monastery but it became much clearer after I went into the desert. There, in seclusion, I so experienced the presence of the Living God that the world was forgotten. There is no way adequately to describe this experience of Divine visitations. They do not repeat themselves in the same form – almost every time they bring something new with a different sequence.

I remember how invocation of the Name Jesus Christ merged with the presence (invisible) of Him Himself. And from that moment this wondrous Name – and other Names of God – have become channels towards unity with Him. At that time I was already an ordained priest. The celebration of the Divine Liturgy likewise assumed a different character: it was not only an act untainted by any wavering of faith but a sensation felt all through me of the FACT of the presence of God, accomplishing the Mystery. I felt the profound meaning and reality contained in St. Basil the Great's words: 'Thou hast given us the revelation of heavenly mysteries.'[x]

[ix] cf. John v: 13.
[x] cf. Liturgy of St. Basil the Great: Offertory Prayer.

Yes, the Lord, even unto us the least of men, reveals the mystery of the priestly service.

After that, my spirit was given to apprehend in many ways the efficacy of the Liturgical Office but I do not know whether I can find words to express my experience. The Liturgy as a Divine Act involves the whole being. There is no querying, HOW is this possible? For the priest it will be obvious, an ontological fact. 'Take – this is My Body . . . Drink – this is My Blood.' And before, I used to take communion, not without faith, not without love, but with a less vivid consciousness of what was happening. Invocation of the Name of Jesus Christ gave me the experience of the blessed – but at the same time fearful – presence of the Eternal God. This does not mean, of course, that a similar sequence is obligatory for everyone.

With the first words of the Liturgy – 'Blessed is the kingdom of the Father, and of the Son, and of the Holy Ghost' – comes God's gracious response. Not always with equal intensity. The Liturgical Canon demands crucial attention. The most exalted moment occurs with the Epiclesis. The priest and with him all who are present in the church petition God the Father to send down the Holy Spirit. And He comes and fulfils their supplication.

Through the Liturgical Act I learned to contemplate the life of Christ-Man. Before saying to the Apostles, 'Take, eat: this is my body'[xi] He had prayed in secret to the Father. He did not utter these fearful words as Master but as the Son of man, teaching us not to allow a single impulse within us that might have a trace of 'self-divinisation'. I have put this conception at the root of my life in Christ. I pray to the Father as a created being. I hope for salvation only as a gift of love from on High. I seek the adoption of sons not otherwise than through Christ; and hallowing and enlightenment only through the Holy Spirit. All these Three – the Father, the Son and

[xi] Mark xiv: 22.

155

the Holy Spirit – according to my profound conception are One Life, One Dominion, One Light, One Love. In Each of them there is absolute Fulness of Divinity. They are separate in me, undivided. They flow together in me without confusion. This is an eternal fact of Divine Being, Whose seal I hunger to receive despite my utter unworthiness. I am not trying to explain the Holy Triunity through logical abstraction. I live this great Mystery reverently, the revelation of which gives me the answer to all my questions.

Our birth and then our development on earth is nothing other than a creative process during the course of which we acquire being to the degree available to us in the hope that knowledge only half gained here will be completed beyond the boundaries of this form of our existence. When all our experiences in our spiritual vision flow together in the single centre of our person; when both sombre hell and Uncreated Light are united in our spirit as a reality which we know, then do we begin to understand the meaning of the Name Jesus – that is, Saviour. He, the Light unoriginate, 'emptied Himself to take on the form of a servant'[xii.] to the point of descending into hell, to deliver Adam therefrom. And now we invoke Him in prayer:

'O Jesus, Son of the Living God, have mercy upon us and upon Thy world.'

The Divine Name, unfolded to people, has served as a link between God and us. Through the Divine Name – better, through the Divine Names – all the sacraments in the Church are performed. Everything must be done in the Divine Name. Through invocation of the Name of the Most-High His presence becomes live, constantly felt. The heart is peaceful when we behave according to the Lord's will. And in every instance of deviation from any aspect whatever of truth the heart feels uncomfortable. In this way prayer effects an

[xii.] cf. Phil. ii: 7.

156

indefatigable inner control over every movement of our spirit. Not a single thought, not a single word escapes it. This practice of continual prayer allows us to cut down our sins to the lowest possible minimum.

'O Lord Jesus Christ, O Son and Word of the Living God, have mercy upon us.'

'Vouchsafe us, O Lord, to live this day without sin.' We pray thus in the morning. But only the gentle presence of the Divine Spirit within us affords us the possibility of continuing sober in spirit. 'No man can say that Jesus is the Lord, but by the Holy Ghost.'[xiii.] Again we see that invoking the Name of the Lord saves us from sinning in deeds and words. 'O Lord Jesus, Thou art Light come to save the world. Lighten the eyes of my heart that without stumbling I may tread my path before Thy Face.'[xiv.]

If our prayers are to lead to results like those of which our Fathers and teachers spoke so rapturously, it is essential that we follow their teaching. The first condition is belief in Christ as God-the-Saviour. The second, to acknowledge ourselves as wretched sinners. This perception can reach such depths that one feels oneself worse than all other men; and this is obvious to us not because of our outer behaviour but because we see how distanced we are from God and recognise ourselves as a potential repository for all evil.

The more we humble ourself in painful repentance, the more rapidly our prayer reaches God. When, though, we lose humility, no ascetic striving will help us. The action in us of pride, criticism of our brethren, self-exalting and hostility towards our neighbour, thrusts us away from the Lord.

We come to God as the worst of sinners. We frankly convict ourselves of every misdeed. We think of nothing, we seek nothing save forgiveness and mercy. This is our invariable

<hr />

[xiii.] I Cor. xii: 3.
[xiv.] cf. John xi: 9–10.

inner state. We beseech God Himself to help us not to grieve the Holy Spirit by our abominable sins; not to let us cause any harm to our brother, to anyone. We condemn ourselves to the torment of hell as unworthy of God. We look for no especial gifts from above, but just try with all our might to perceive the true import of Christ's commandments and live according to them. We appeal to Him:

'O Lord Jesus Christ, have mercy upon us and upon Thy world.'

And God hears us, and brings us salvation. 'And whosoever shall call on the name of the Lord [in a similar spirit] shall be delivered.'[xv.]

'Repent.'[xvi.] We must heed this injunction of Christ's carefully, radically amend our inner life and our concept of the world; our attitude towards people and every phenomenon in the creature world; not slay our enemies but win them over with love. We must remember that there is no absolute evil. Only unoriginate Goodness is Absolute. And this Goodness commanded us, 'Love your enemies . . . do good to them that hate you . . . Be ye perfect, even as your Father which is in heaven is perfect.'[xvii.] Being slain for the sake of one's brethren is the best possible weapon for delivering them from servitude to the traducer, the devil, and preparing their souls to accept God, Who desires the salvation of all. There is no one in whom there is no light whatever, because God 'lighteth every man that cometh into the world.'[xviii.] The commandment 'Resist not evil'[xix.] is the most fully effective form of struggle against evil. When we resort to the same means adopted by those who do wrong, the dynamics of world-evil increase. Slaughter of the innocent in an invisible fashion often transfers the moral powers of mankind to the

[xv.] Joel ii: 32.
[xvi.] Matt. iv: 17.
[xvii.] Matt. v: 44, 48.
[xviii.] John i: 9.
[xix.] Matt. v: 39.

side of the good for which the innocent died. It is not so when both sides evince the same bad tendency to dominate. Victory obtained by physical strength does not last for ever. God being light holy and pure withdraws from evil-doers and they fall away from the one and only source of life, and die. 'Dearly beloved, avenge not yourselves, but rather give place unto wrath: for it is written, Vengeance is mine; I will repay, saith the Lord . . . Be not overcome of evil, but overcome evil with good.'[xx.]

People, bearers of only relative truth, in their fanatical struggle to have their ideas triumph dismantle the wholeness of being, and in the end destroy everything. In their short-sightedness they make absolute the positive aspect of their political doctrine and are ready to dismiss all those who would like to see the life of the universe based on more humane principles – most of all, of course, on the commandments of Christ, slain for His preaching of love. In the contemporary world the Gospel words of Christ assume a particularly topical character: '. . . Ye shall hear of wars and rumours of wars: see that ye be not troubled: for all these things must come to pass . . . and ye [Christians] shall be hated of all nations for my name's sake . . . And because iniquity shall abound, the love of many shall wax cold . . . and then shall the end come.'[xxi.]

'O Lord Jesus Christ, Son of God, have mercy upon us and upon Thy world.'

The whole world is split by dissension – between states with different social structures; between races and classes; between different faiths and ideologies. *Et al.* With contemporary facilities for massive destruction and annihilation everyone, everywhere, lives in an atmosphere of fear, 'looking after those things which are coming on the earth.'[xxii.] And here we are faced with a tissue of paradoxes difficult to

[xx.] Rom. xii: 19, 21.
[xxi.] Matt. xxiv: 6–14.
[xxii.] Luke xxi: 26.

resolve. For the one part we cannot continue untroubled since we belong to the human family with many moments of fate in common. On the other, there are the words of Christ: 'When these things begin to come to pass, then look up, and lift up your heads; for your redemption draweth nigh.'[xxiii] We need not linger here to make a more detailed description of the state of already existing apocalyptic tension; but we will not let go of the powerful weapon that the Lord gave us – PRAYER.

'O Lord Jesus Christ, Son of the Living God, have mercy upon us and Thy world.'

Nor, so long as it remains practically possible, celebration of the Liturgical sacrifice.

'. . . And the Lord God formed man of the dust of the ground, and breathed into his nostrils the breath of life; and man became a living soul.'[xxiv] And we are drawn to Him parched with thirst to be united with Him eternally. And He Himself awaits us with love. Thirst for God imbues our earthly being and we mean to die so. Christ Himself dying on the cross cried, 'I thirst.'[xxv] He 'hungered', too:[xxvi] and thirsted, and was 'straitened'[xxvii] that we should know the Father. And we, also, are straitened on earth, grieved by the nightmarish, uninterrupted spectacle of violence, slaughter, hatred, and we thirst to go to the Father, and we invoke the Name of His only-begotten Son:

'O Lord Jesus Christ, Son of God, have mercy upon us.'

'Then opened he their understanding, that they might understand the scriptures, And said unto them, Thus it is written, and thus it behoved Christ to suffer, and to rise from the dead the third day: And that REPENTANCE . . .

[xxiii] Luke xxi: 28.
[xxiv] Gen. ii: 7.
[xxv] John xix: 28.
[xxvi] Matt. xxi: 18.
[xxvii] cf. Luke xii: 50.

should be preached IN HIS NAME among all nations.'[xxviii.]
If His Name gives us the joy of knowing the mysteries of
the love of the Unoriginate for us, then, of course we love
His very Name, too. In It is contained 'the fellowship of the
mystery, which from the beginning of the world hath been
hid in God, who created all things by Jesus Christ . . . who
hath chosen us in him before the foundation of the world,
that we should be holy and without blame before him in
love: Having predestinated us unto the adoption of children
by Jesus Christ to himself.'[xxix.]

Prayer over the years so transforms our fallen nature that
it becomes possible for it to be sanctified through the Truth
revealed to us. And this before we depart from this world.[xxx.]

'O Lord Jesus, have mercy upon us.'

The measureless grandeur of the task set before us instils fear
in us. We are told that 'the kingdom of heaven suffereth
violence, and the violent take it by force.'[xxxi.] Long-continuing ascetic effort will show that in the Gospel revelation
everything relates to another loftier plane. The blinding Light
of Divinity is reflected on our plane as the commandment,
'Love your enemies . . . Be ye therefore perfect, even as your
Father . . . is perfect.'[xxxii.] Only the indwelling in us of Him
Who gave this commandment will help us to fulfil this
command. Wherefore our cry to Him:

'O Lord Jesus Christ, Son of the Living God, have mercy
upon us.'

Invocation of the Lord's Name gradually unites us with Him.
This can happen to a certain degree when the one who is
praying does not yet understand 'WHO this is,'[xxxiii.] and so

---

[xxviii.] Luke xxiv: 45–47.
[xxix.] cf. Eph. i: 4–5; iii: 9.
[xxx.] cf. John xvii: 17.
[xxxi.] Matt. xi: 12.
[xxxii.] Matt. v: 44, 48.
[xxxiii.] cf. Matt. xxi: 10.

far only vaguely senses the sanctifying power that proceeds from the Name. Every step forward, however, without fail entails an ever-deepening recognition of our sinfulness which reduces us to despair. Then with ever-increasing energy we invoke the wondrous Name:

'O Jesus, my Saviour, have mercy upon me.'

Sacred tradition, our most precious inheritance from the Lord Himself through the Apostles and Fathers of the Church, teaches us to continue in spiritual poverty, in recognition of the presence in us of sinful death, if we really aspire to persevere in truth. 'If we say that we have no sin, we deceive ourselves, and the truth is not in us. If we confess our sins, he is faithful and just to forgive us our sins, and to cleanse us from all unrighteousness. If we say that we have not sinned, we make him a liar, and his word is not in us.'[xxxiv]

'O Lord, Jesus Christ, have mercy upon me, a sinner.'

With the same tension – and sometimes even worse – that people live in who are stricken by a deadly illness (cancer, for instance) so do others experience the presence in them of sinful passions separating them from the Lord. They do truly acknowledge themselves 'the worst of all men', genuinely see themselves in outer darkness. Then they summon up within them the utmost energy of prayer-repentance. Repentance can reach such a degree that their minds come to a halt and they find no words other than

'Jesus, save me, a sinner.'

It is salutary for us if aversion to sin so increases in us that it turns into detestation of oneself. Otherwise, we are in danger of getting used to sin, which is so many-sided and subtle that generally we do not even notice its presence in all our deeds, which may even seem to be good. It is a difficult but splendid ascetic feat to plunge our sovereign mind down to

---

[xxxiv] I John i: 8–10.

the invisible centre of our person by the invocation of the Name of Jesus Christ, without faith in Whom none of us can see the fatal poison of sin active in us. Through this kind of struggle against the evil within us, not only the depths of our own being but the mysterious abysses of cosmic life, too, will be opened to us. Then our spirit will turn away from the petty and superficial phenomena of everyday life and 'appalled' by oneself recognise the holy force of another prayer, of another plane, crying:

'O Lord, Jesus my Saviour, have mercy upon me, accursed one.'

Concerning prayer in the Name of Jesus Christ the Epistles and the works of the Holy Fathers can be quoted. For instance, Prayer is a 'consuming fire'[xxxv] — consuming our passions. It is light, enlightening our mind, making it perspicacious and long-sighted, able to see all that is happening within us. We can speak of it in the words of the Epistle to the Hebrews: 'It is quick, and powerful, and sharper than any twoedged sword, piercing even to the dividing asunder of soul and spirit, and of the joints and marrow, and is a discerner of the thoughts and intents of the heart. Neither is there any creature that is not manifest in his sight: but ALL THINGS ARE NAKED AND OPENED' in its light.[xxxvi]

Praying this prayer brings man to encounter many forces hidden in the 'Cosmos'. It provokes these cosmic forces — 'the rulers of the darkness of this world . . . spiritual wickedness in high places'[xxxvii] — into fierce hostility. Victory, however, comes with repentance to the point of 'hatred for his own life.'[xxxviii] The book of The Revelation of St. John the Divine describes this kind of battle. 'They overcame him [the Devil, and Satan, which deceiveth the whole world]

[xxxv] Heb. xii: 29.
[xxxvi] cf. Heb. iv: 12, 13.
[xxxvii] Eph. vi: 12.
[xxxviii] cf. Luke xiv: 26.

by the blood of the Lamb, and by the word of their testimony; and they *loved not their lives unto the death.*[xxxix]

Prayer of burning repentance lifts the spirit into spheres that lie over the frontiers of the 'wisdom of the wise of this world.'[xl] It is awesome to speak of this prayer which first takes one through the black depths of outer darkness hidden within us and then unites into one our spirit and the Divine Spirit, and allows us while we are still here to live holy eternity. All through the centuries the Fathers have been astounded by the magnificence of this gift to the fallen world:

'O Lord, Jesus Christ, Who only art holy,
Who alone art the true Saviour of all men,
Have mercy upon us and upon Thy world.'

The beauty of the created world delights us but at the same time our spirit is still more strongly attracted to the imperishable beauty of the Unoriginate Divine Being. With striking clarity the Lord Jesus let us see the celestial light of the Heavenly Kingdom. Contemplation of this splendour releases us from the consequences of the Fall, and the grace of the Holy Spirit restores in us the primordial image and likeness of God, as manifest to us by Christ in our flesh. And now invocation of His Name is our continual prayer:

'O Lord Jesus Christ, our Saviour, have mercy upon us and upon Thy world.'

This prayer in its final implementation unites us altogether with Christ. With it the human hypostasis is not lost in the Divine Being, like a drop of water in the ocean. Man's personality is indestructible in eternity. 'I AM; I am ... the truth, and the life.' 'I am the light of the world.'[xli] Being, Truth, Light are not abstract concepts, impersonal substances – not 'WHAT' but 'WHO'. Where there is no personal

[xxxix] Revelation xii: 11, 9.
[xl] cf. I Cor. i: 19–20.
[xli] John viii: 58; xiv: 6; ix: 5.

164

form of being, there is nothing alive either, just as there is neither good nor evil there; neither light nor darkness. Briefly, there can be nothing. 'Without him was not any thing made that was made. In him was life.'[xlii]

'O Lord Jesus Christ, Son of the Living God,
Have mercy upon us and upon Thy world.'

When invocation of the Name of Jesus is coupled with the coming of the Uncreated Light the significance of this Name is made particularly plain to us. Then can we experience 'the kingdom of God come with power'[xliii] and the spirit of him who is praying detects the Father's voice, saying, 'This is my beloved Son: hear him.'[xliii] And we pray:

'O Lord Jesus Christ, Only-begotten Son of the Father,
Have mercy upon us, and save us.'

Christ showed us the Father in Himself: 'He that hath seen me hath seen the Father.'[xliv] Now we know the Father in the measure in which we have known the Son: 'I and the Father are one.'[xlv] And so, the Son reveals the Father, and the Father bears witness to the Son, and we pray:

'Only-begotten Son of God,
Have mercy upon us, and save Thy world.'

'All things are delivered unto me of my Father: and no man knoweth the Son, but the Father; neither knoweth any man the Father, save the Son, and he to whomsoever the Son will reveal Him.'[xlvi] And the Son we know only insofar as we abide in the spirit of His commandments. Without Him we are powerless to rise to the heights commanded of

[xlii] John i: 3–4.
[xliii] Mark ix: 1, 7.
[xliv] John xiv: 9.
[xlv] John x: 30.
[xlvi] Matt. xi: 27.

us, since the commandments reveal the life of God Himself. Hence our cry to Him:

'O Lord Jesus Christ, Son Unoriginate with the Father, have mercy upon me. Come unto me, and make Thine abode in me, together with the Father and the Holy Spirit, according to Thy promise.[xlvii] . . . O Lord, O Jesus, have mercy upon me, a sinner.'

In the Old Testament the Name of the Father was known but He was perceived in the obscurity of incomprehensibility. It was Christ Who manifested the Father to us in the utmost detail in Himself. He revealed the true range of all that was given before Him through Moses and the Prophets. 'I am in the Father, and the Father in me . . . I and my Father are one . . . I have declared unto them thy name, and will declare it [fully]: that the love wherewith thou hast loved me may be in them, and I in them.'[xlviii] Knowing the Name of the Father means knowing also of His, the Father's, love for us. Invocation of the Name of Jesus leads us into the sphere of Divine Life, and the Father, and the Son, and the Holy Spirit are given to us in the Name of Jesus:

'O Lord Jesus Christ, Son of God, have mercy upon us and upon Thy world.'

Invoking the Name of Jesus with the fullest possible perception of what it contains in itself means already being completely in unity with God of the Holy Trinity. This God revealed Himself to us in His new relation to man — not now as Creator but as Saviour of the world; as Light of Truth and true eternity:

'O Lord Jesus Christ, Son of the Pre-Eternal Father, have mercy upon us.'

The theology of the Name and the theology of the ikon

[xlvii] cf. John xiv: 23.
[xlviii] John xiv: 11; x: 30; xvii: 26.

have many traits in common. Contemplating the ikon of Christ, in spirit we rise into contact with Him. We confess His manifestation in the flesh — He is both God and man, wholly man and perfect Divine likeness. We go further than colours and outlines into the world of the intelligence and the spirit. So it is that in invoking the Name we do not linger on the sound but live its content. The sound may change according to the different languages used but the content — cognition — contained in the Name remains immutable.

'O Lord, Jesus Christ, save us.'

Invocation voiced aloud of the Divine Name by itself is not enough. 'Not every one that saith unto me, Lord, Lord, shall enter into the kingdom of heaven; but he that doeth the will of my Father which is in heaven. Many will say to me in that day, Lord, Lord, have we not prophesied in thy name? and in thy name have cast out devils? and in thy name done many wonderful works? And then will I profess unto them, I never knew you: depart from me, ye that work iniquity.'[xlix] It is not easy for us to hear these words — Divine justice is a dreadful affair.

'O Lord Jesus, have mercy and save me, a sinner.'

Knowing that through Christ we have received 'the adoption of sons,'[l] we shall glorify Him Who created us. Invoking the Name of Jesus Christ, we shall give Him to resound in us with the strength and majesty proper to Him. May it annihilate the roots of sin living in us. May it strike the flames of His love in our stony hearts. May it give us light and understanding. May it make us communicants in His glory. May His peace which passeth all understanding[li] through His Name be implanted in us. After long years of the Jesus

---

[xlix] Matt. vii: 21–23.
[l] cf. Gal. iv: 5.
[li] cf. John xiv: 27; Phil. iv: 7.

Prayer may God grant us to know the fulness of revelation contained in it: 'Wonderful, Counsellor, The mighty God, The everlasting Father, The Prince of Peace, the Lord of hosts.'[lii.]

'O Lord Jesus Christ, Son of the Living God, have mercy upon us, and upon Thy world.'

In humility must we invoke the Divine Name. Christ, Master of the universe, was made flesh and as man humbled Himself even unto death on the cross. Wherefore His Name is above every name that is named, not only in this world, but also in that which is to come. The Father 'set him at his own right hand in the heavenly places . . . And gave him to be the head over all things to the church, Which is his body, the fulness of him that filleth all in all.'[liii.]

'O Lord Jesus Christ our God, have mercy upon us and upon Thy Church, and Thy world, by the prayers of the Mother of God, of the Holy Apostles and of all Thy saints down the ages.'

The way of our Fathers requires strong faith and long-suffering, whereas our contemporaries attempt to acquire spiritual gifts, including even direct contemplation of the Absolute God, through pressure and in a brief space of time. Often one can remark a disposition in them to draw a parallel between prayer in the Name of Jesus and yoga or 'transcendental meditation' and the like. I think it necessary to point out the dangers of this delusion – the danger of looking on prayer as a very simple, easy 'technical' means leading to direct union with God. I consider it essential to emphasise the radical difference between the Jesus Prayer and all other ascetic theories. All those are deluded who endeavour mentally to divest themselves of everything that is transitory, relative, in order in this way to cross some invisible threshold,

[lii.] Isa. ix: 6; viii: 18; Acts iv: 12.
[liii.] cf. Eph. i: 20–23.

to realise their being 'without beginning', their 'identity' with the Source of all that is; in order to return to Him, to be merged in Him, the nameless trans-personal Absolute; in order in the vast expanse of what is beyond thought to unify one's personal individuality with the individualised form of natural existence. Ascetic efforts of this kind enabled some strugglers to a certain extent to rise to meta-logical contemplation of being; to experience a certain awe; to know the state when the mind is stilled, when it goes beyond the bounds of time and space. In like states man may feel the peace of divestment of the constantly changing manifestations of the visible world: may uncover in himself freedom of spirit and contemplate mental beauty.

The ultimate development of such impersonal asceticism has led many ascetics to perceive the divine origin in the very nature of man; to a tendency to the self-divinisation that lay at the root of the great Fall; to see in man a certain 'absoluteness' which in essence is nothing else but the reflection of the Divine Absoluteness in the creature created in His likeness; to feel drawn to return to the state of peace which man knew before his appearance in this world. In any case after this experience of divesture some such form of mental aberration may arise in the mind. I am not setting myself the task of listing all the various types of mental intuition but I will say from my own experience that the True, Living God – the I AM – is *not* here in all this. This is the natural genius of the human spirit in his sublimated impulses towards the Absolute. All contemplation arrived at by this means is self-contemplation, not contemplation of God. In these circumstances we open up for ourselves created beauty, not First-Being. And in all of it there is no salvation for man.

The source of real deliverance lies in unquestionable, wholehearted acceptance of the Revelation, 'I am that I am . . . I am Alpha and Omega, the first and the last.'[liv] God

[liv] Exod. iii: 14; Rev. i: 11.

is Personal Absolute, Trinity One and Indivisible. Our whole Christian life is based on this Revelation. This God called us from non-being into life. Knowledge of this Living God and discernment of the manner of His creation releases us from the obscurity of our own ideas, coming 'from beneath,'[lv.] about the Absolute; rescues us from our attraction – unconscious but for all that ruinous – to withdrawal from existence of any sort. We are created in order to be communicants in the Divine Being of Him Who really is. Christ indicated this wondrous way: 'Strait is the gate, and narrow is the way, which leadeth unto life.'[lvi.] Apprehending the depths of the Creator's wisdom, we embark on the suffering through which Divine eternity is to be attained. And when His Light shines for us we unite in ourselves contemplation of the two extremes of the abyss – on the one side, the darkness of hell, on the other, the triumph of victory. We are existentially introduced into the province of Uncreated Divine Life. And hell loses power over us. We are given grace – to live the state of the Incarnate Logos-Christ Who descended into hell as Conqueror. Then by the power of His love we shall embrace all creation in the prayer:

'O Jesus, Gracious Almighty, have mercy upon us and Thy world.'

Revelation of this Personal God imparts a wondrous character to all things. Being is not some determined cosmic process but the Light of the indescribable love between Divine and created persons. It is the free movement of spirits filled with wise knowledge of all that exists, and consciousness of self. Without this there is no sense in anything but only death. But our prayer becomes a living contact of our created *persona* and the Divine Person – that is, something absolute. And this is expressed when we address the Word of the Father:

[lv.] cf. John viii: 23.
[lvi.] Matt. vii: 14.

'O Lord Jesus Christ, Unoriginate Word of Thine Unoriginate Father, have mercy upon us. Save us and Thy world.'

Beginning to understand the wise plan for us of our Creator and God stimulates our love for Him, and we are newly inspired in our prayer. Contemplation of Divine Wisdom in the beauty of the world attracts our spirit to fresh heights, detaching us from all earthly matters. This detachment is not some hovering in the sphere of pure ideas, however attractive they may appear to us. Nor are they artistic-poetic creation but the absolute seizure of all our earthly energy by some hitherto unknown life. The Gospel lifts our spirit higher than all creature life – the Gospel in which we begin to perceive the Act of Divine Self-revelation. This means introduction into the grace of theology not as some scholastic science but as a state of communion with God. We do not subject the Lord's Word to our inferior judgment but judge us ourselves in the light of our given knowledge. In our then natural urge to make the Gospel word the substance of our whole being we release ourselves from the power over us of the passions, and with the strength of God-Jesus vanquish the cosmic evil lodged in us. We effectively cognise that He, Jesus, is the sole, in the proper sense, Saviour-God, and Christian prayer is unceasing invocation of His Name:

'O Lord Jesus Christ, Son of God and God, have mercy upon us and Thy world.'

The big question confronting all mankind with a tragic problem is this: Where lies true Being, and where the mirage of our fallen imagination? Where indeed is living eternity, and where the illusory attraction of our spirit towards ideas which we can perceive through our own intelligence? Is the principle of the person-hypostasis limited *ipso facto* and therefore unworthy of, and inapplicable to, God, or is this very principle the image of the Living Absolute: I AM THAT I AM? Our whole future depends on the answer we give. If we decide that the principle of the person is *per se* restricting, then our ascetic effort will be concentrated on transcending this principle in ourselves. And vice versa − if we apprehend it as the only possible image of Absolute Being, enraptured by the power flowing into us we shall pray: 'Our Father, which art in heaven . . .' or 'O Lord Jesus Christ, Son of the Father, have mercy upon us. Take us into Thy life healing us from every trace of sin that destroys us.' If the immortality pledged to us in Christ through resurrection means a personal resurrection, then in no wise would we 'be unclothed, but clothed upon, that mortality might be swallowed up of life. Now he that hath wrought us for the selfsame thing is God, who also hath given unto us the earnest of the Spirit.'[lvii.]

'O Christ Jesus, risen from the dead, have mercy upon us.'

'If ye believe not that I am he [Who was revealed to Moses on Sinai], ye shall die in your sins.'[lviii.] 'Abraham rejoiced to see my day: and he saw it, and was glad.'[lix.] 'I appeared unto Abraham, unto Isaac, and unto Jacob, by the name of God Almighty, but by my name JEHOVAH was I not known to them.'[lx.] 'For had ye believed Moses, ye would have believed me: for he wrote of me.'[lxi.] 'And beginning at Moses and all the prophets, he expounded unto them in all the scriptures the things concerning himself.'[lxii.] Thus in our spiritual death we have lost the feeling of sin and now without Christ and the grace of the Holy Spirit we cannot detect sin in us. For sin is essentially always an offence against Divine love. This transgression is only possible if 'I AM' − that is God − is Absolutely Personal, and relations with Him are profoundly personal. There is no other faith, no other religion where

[lvii.] II Cor. v: 4−5.
[lviii.] John viii: 24.
[lix.] John viii: 56.
[lx.] Exod. vi: 3; cf. Acts vii: 2.
[lxi.] John v: 46.
[lxii.] Luke xxiv: 27.

the mystery of sin is so clearly exposed. We have St. Ephraim of Syria, filled with the Holy Spirit, praying: 'Vouchsafe that I may see my sins.' And all the Fathers used to say that to see one's sin meant more than any apparition of Angels. Thus it is that we, discerning what has been hidden since the beginning of time, cry with softened heart,

'O Lord Jesus Christ, have mercy upon me, a sinner, and save me who am fallen.'

'Great is the mystery of godliness: God was manifest in the flesh, justified in the Spirit, seen of angels, preached unto the Gentiles, believed on in the world, received up into glory.'[lxiii.] We are all successors to Adam who fell like Lucifer. To the one created in the Divine image, the idea of divinisation comes naturally. The question is, how to achieve this purpose, this mission. If we are created beings and not First and Self-Beings, it is preposterous to suppose that we can become 'equal' to God, bypassing Him.

Our life is based on 'the appearance of God in the flesh'. If belief in our divinisation is imprescriptable for us, then the way to divinisation lies in adoption of the life of God Who manifested Himself to us in our form of existence. We must indeed absorb His word, His Spirit, into ourselves — become like Him in all our manifestations. And the more complete our likeness to Him in this world, the fuller and more perfect our divinisation. St. Paul says, 'He that is joined' (through prayer and communion) 'unto the Lord is one spirit'[lxiv.] and so we pray:

'O Lord Jesus Christ, only-begotten Son of the Father, Thou art our hope. With Thee and through Thee lead us to the Father . . . Have mercy upon me, a sinner.'

Eternal life in the bosom of the Holy Trinity — that is the purport of the summons. But this 'kingdom suffereth vio-

[lxiii.] I Tim. iii: 16.
[lxiv.] I Cor. vi: 17.

lence, and the violent take it by force.'[lxv.] Self-constraint is imperative 'because strait is the gate, and narrow is the way, which leadeth unto life, and few there be that find it.'[lxvi.] And when we Christians refuse to go along with those who 'do not find it', because they do not want it, conflict arises. We become unwelcome sons of this world. Such is the lot of those who love Christ. When the Lord is with us all our suffering in this world no longer terrifies, because with Him we have passed from death into life. But hours – long periods even – of being forsaken by God are inevitable. 'My God, my God, why hast thou forsaken me?'[lxvii.] And if with this we are rejected by other people our despair may go very deep indeed, and we cry unto Him Who Himself was tempted and so is 'able to succour them that are tempted:'[lxviii.]

'O Lord Jesus, save me, I sink, as Thou didst save Peter.'[lxix.]

In the ascetic feat of prayer we each of us go as far as is possible for us. It is not easy to find oneself or to define the limits of our strength. Those who are led by the Holy Spirit never cease condemning themselves as unworthy of God. In moments of deep despair they do move away for a while from the brink of the abyss where they stand in spirit, in order to allow mind and body a breathing-space before returning anew to the abyss. But whether he rests or whether in a peaceful period, there always remains a sort of wound in the depths of the ascetic's heart, which does not allow him to lapse into proud ideas about himself. Ascetic humility becomes more and more rooted in his soul, becomes characteristic, as it were. Sorrow and sickness are the nature of our earthly progression. Otherwise, none of the sons of Adam would keep up in humility. But those who do endure are

[lxv.] Matt. xi: 12.
[lxvi.] Matt. vii: 14.
[lxvii.] Matt. xxvii: 46.
[lxviii.] Heb. ii: 18.
[lxix.] cf. Matt. xiv: 30.

vouchsafed the gift of Christ-like humility,[lxx.] which Staretz Silouan says is 'indescribable' for it belongs to another, higher plane of being. Acquisition of this gift is only possible through constant thinking of Christ and prayer to Him:

'O Lord Jesus Christ, Great and Holy God, Do Thou Thyself teach me Thy humility . . . I pray Thee, have mercy upon me, a sinner.'

So then, our nature can be recast only in the fire of repentance. Only tearful prayer will destroy the roots of passion in us. Only invocation of the Name of Jesus can cleanse, regenerate and hallow our nature. 'Now ye are clean through the word which I have spoken unto you. Abide in me . . .'[lxxi.] And how are we to abide? You are given My Name, and 'whatsoever ye shall ask of the Father in my name, he may give it to you.'[lxxii.]

'O Lord Jesus Christ Who only art without sin, have mercy upon me, a sinner.'

Our fathers exhort us to pray the Name of Jesus, not altering the formula very often. But, on the other hand, this is imperative in order to renew our attention, reinforce our prayer even, when the mind moves into theological contemplation or the heart expands to embrace the whole world. Thus by the Name of Christ Jesus it is possible to cover every inside and outside event. Thus this wondrous prayer becomes all-embracing, universal.

[lxx.] cf. Matt. xi: 29.
[lxxi.] John xv: 3; xvii: 17.
[lxxii.] John xv: 16.

PRAYERS

O Heavenly King and Comforter,
Spirit of Truth,
Treasure of Goodness and Giver of Life –

Come and abide in us,
Guide us into all truth,
And save our souls, O Thou Who art Good.

PRAYER AT DAYBREAK

O Lord Eternal and Creator of all things,
Who of Thine inscrutable goodness didst call me to this
    life;
Who didst bestow on me the grace of Baptism
and the Seal of the Holy Spirit;
Who hast imbued me with the desire to seek Thee,
the one true God: hear my prayer.

I have no life, no light, no joy or wisdom;
no strength except in Thee, O God.
Because of my unrighteousness I dare not raise my eyes to
    Thee.
But Thou didst say to Thy disciples,
'Whatsoever ye shall ask in prayer believing, ye shall receive'
and 'Whatsoever ye shall ask in my name, that will I do'.
Wherefore I dare to invoke Thee.
Purify me from all taint of flesh and spirit.
Teach me to pray aright.

Bless this day which Thou dost give unto me,
Thine unworthy servant. By the power of Thy blessing
enable me at all times to speak and act to Thy glory
with a pure spirit, with humility, patience, love,
gentleness, peace, courage and wisdom:
aware always of Thy presence.

Of Thine immense goodness, O Lord God, shew me the
    path of Thy will,
and grant me to walk in Thy sight without sin.

O Lord, unto Whom all hearts be open,
Thou knowest what things I have need of.
Thou art acquainted with my blindness and my ignorance,
Thou knowest my infirmity and my soul's corruption;
but neither are my pain and anguish hid from Thee.

Wherefore I beseech Thee, hear my prayer
and by Thy Holy Spirit teach me the way wherein I should
walk;
and when my perverted will would lead me down other
paths
spare me not, O Lord, but force me back to Thee.
By the power of Thy love, grant me to hold fast to that
which is good.
Preserve me from every word or deed that corrupts the
soul;
from every impulse unpleasing in Thy sight
and hurtful to my brother-man.
Teach me what I should say and *how* I should speak.
If it be Thy will that I make no answer,
inspire me to keep silent in a spirit of peace
that causeth neither sorrow nor hurt to my fellow.
Establish me in the path of Thy commandments
and to my last breath let me not stray from the light of
Thine ordinances,
that Thy commandments may become the sole law of my
being
on this earth and in all eternity.

Yea, Lord, I pray Thee, have pity on me.
Spare me in mine affliction and my misery
and hide not the way of salvation from me.

In my foolishness, O God, I plead with Thee for many and
great things.
Yet am I ever mindful of my wickedness, my baseness, my
vileness.
Have mercy upon me.
Cast me not away from Thy presence because of my
presumption.
Do Thou rather increase in me this presumption,
and grant unto me, the worst of men,
to love Thee as Thou hast commanded,

with all my heart, and with all my soul,
and with all my mind, and with all my strength:
with my whole being.

Yea, O Lord, by Thy Holy Spirit,
teach me good judgment and knowledge.
Grant me to know Thy truth before I go down into the
  grave.
Maintain my life in this world until I may offer unto Thee
  worthy repentance.
Take me not away in the midst of my days,
nor while my mind is still blind.
When Thou shalt be pleased to bring my life to an end,
forewarn me that I may prepare my soul to come before
  Thee.
Be with me, O Lord, at that dread hour
and grant me the joy of salvation.
Cleanse Thou me from secret faults,
from all iniquity that is hid in me;
and give me a right answer before Thy judgment-seat.

Yea, Lord, of Thy great mercy
and immeasurable love for mankind,

Hear my prayer.

EVENING AND MORNING PRAYERS

I. O LORD unoriginate, invisible, searchless; immutable, constant, invincible; Who only hast immortality, dwelling in light inaccessible; Who in Thine ineffable wisdom didst create every living thing; and didst summon us from the night of non-being into life with Thee; Who didst give us to know Thee, the One true God; Who hast enabled us Thy sinful and unworthy servants to stand before Thy Face, confessing ourselves and bringing unto Thee, our God, our [morning/evening] praise: Do Thou Thyself, O Master that art loving-kind, direct our prayer as incense before Thee, and let it be as sweet spice; and vouchsafe unto us grace and strength to sing unto Thee reasonably, and to pray unceasing prayer in fear and trembling enacting our salvation.

Yea, O Lord our God, hear us at this hour, and crush underfoot our invisible and warring enemies. For Thine it is to pardon and save us, and to Thee alone we render glory, to the Father, and to the Son, and to the Holy Spirit; now, and for ever: world without end. Amen.

II. O Great and wondrous GOD, Who of Thy searchless mercy and rich providence dost govern all things, and hast granted unto us the good things of this world; Who hast preserved us even unto this day and hour, and verily prepared for us the promised kingdom: Of Thy goodness vouchsafe that we may live the remainder of our lives undefiled before Thy face, and worthily hymn Thee, the One True God.

For Thou it was Who didst create and bring us into this life. Thou it is that dost shew us the way to salvation, and hast granted unto us the revelation of heavenly mysteries. Thou didst set us to this office by Thy Holy Spirit. Whereby we pray Thee: Look down on us now, and accept these our unworthy supplications, as a pure and pleasing sacrifice before Thee; and cleansing us from all filthiness of flesh and spirit, from every sin and iniquity concealed in us, send down on us Thy grace; and may Thy mercy be imprescriptible and constant. Let us not be for a reproach, and a mocking to our enemies.

For Thou, O Lord, Who knowest all things ere we ask of Thee, dost see our shame and our ignominy, our lowliness and affliction. Come, and by Thy strength crush them that contend against us.

Yea, O Lord, enter not into judgment with Thy servants. Remember rather the infirmity of our flesh, and for Thy goodness' sake, come and dwell in us, working in us that which is wellpleasing in Thy sight, that rejoicing we may ever hymn Thy glory, of the Father, and of the Son, and of the Holy Spirit.

III. O Great and eternal GOD, the One true and righteous God, bountiful, and gracious: May Thy Spirit come down to us, and Thy strength overshadow us. From Thy holy dwelling-place stretch forth Thine unseen hand, and bless us every one. And of Thy goodness grant that we may continue steadfast in the ways of Thy will, and even unto our last breath ever cover us with Thine immeasurable loving-kindness in every place of Thy ruling. Thou only art the protection and all-powerful defender of our life, and we ascribe glory to Thee, to the Father, and to the Son, and to the Holy Ghost; now, and for ever: world without end. Amen.

IV. O GOD, our GOD, Who hast vouchsafed to gather us at this hour for prayer: Grant unto us Thy grace that our mouths may be opened. And teach us to pray unto Thee, for we know not what is befitting unless Thou, O Lord, by Thy Holy Spirit instruct us and teach us. Wherefore we beseech Thee, have mercy upon us, forgive us our trespasses, voluntary and involuntary, whether of word or deed or thought, witting or unwitting: For Thou art good and loving-kind. Thou art the God of them that repent,

and unto Thee we ascribe glory and thanksgiving, unto
the Father, and unto the Son, and unto the Holy Spirit;
now, and for ever: world without end. Amen.

V. O LORD our GOD, Whose dominion is ineffable,
Whose glory is searchless, and mercy without measure;
Whose loving-kindness is inexpressible: Do Thou, O
Master most-holy, fulfil our petitions as be expedient unto
us, and work for us Thy rich mercy and bounteous
kindness. Guide us to the harbour of Thy will. Open the
eyes of our hearts to knowledge of Thy truth. Preserve us
from every false path, and from the manifold snares of the
devil, and keep our whole life in safety by the grace of
Thine All-holy Spirit. Set an angel of peace to guide our
goings out and our comings in to every good thing, and
grant us, O God, our God, faith unashamed, hope
unfailing, love without dissimulation. Implant in us Thy
holy and life-giving fear. Tell us of the joy of Thy salvation,
and by Thy sovereign Spirit confirm us in Thy love.
Vouchsafe that even unto our last breath we may bring
Thee the sacrifice of truth, and praise undefiled, together
with all Thy creatures. For all the heavenly Powers do
hymn Thee, and unto Thee we ascribe glory, unto the
Father, and unto the Son, and unto the Holy Spirit; now,
and for ever: world without end. Amen.

VI. O GOD our CREATOR, look down on Thy sinful
and unworthy servants, and when we are called to venerate
Thy holy Name deprive us not of the hope of Thy mercy.
Grant unto us, O Lord, all that be needful for salvation, and
vouchsafe that we may love and fear Thee with our whole
heart, and in all things work Thy will. For Thou art our
God, ever hymned and magnified with ceaseless song by all
the heavenly hosts. Let our mouths likewise be filled with
Thy praise for the majesty of Thy holy Name. And grant
us to participate and inherit with all them that fear Thee
in truth, and keep Thy commandments. By the prayers of

the all-holy Mother of God and ever-Virgin Mary, by the intercessions of the heavenly, incorporeal powers, and of all Thy saints down the ages.

For unto Thee belong all glory, honour and worship, unto the Father, and unto the Son, and unto the Holy Ghost; now, and for ever: world without end. Amen.

VII. O HOLY KING, Jesus Christ, Son unoriginate of the Father without beginning; O Word, Who created and brought us into this life, and of Thy measureless good will didst clothe us in this flesh; and in the infirmity of our nature didst manifest to us the searchless image of the Father; and by the sending down from heaven of the Holy Spirit gave us the revelation of heavenly mysteries, and made us partakers of Thine ineffable light: Receive us now who bow down before Thee, and forgive us our trespasses, voluntary and involuntary. Of Thy strength heal our every infirmity, and by Thy providence defend us in the coming times of our life, the which Thou didst deign to grant unto Thine unworthy servants; and bless our every deed and word, our comings in and our goings out in our every good undertaking. By Thy Holy Spirit set us on the paths of Thy commandments, and make us steadfast in the confession of Thy word. Grant unto us, and unto Thy holy Church, peace unashamed and inviolable. Stablish brotherly love and concord in Thy whole world.

VIII. O LORD JESUS CHRIST, our SAVIOUR, Who didst grant Thy peace unto man, and didst send down from heaven the gift of Thy Most Holy Spirit for an imprescriptible inheritance to the faithful; by His supernal working the imperishable light of knowledge of God was granted to the human race, and we were delivered from temptation as from the darkness of false allures, and were enlightened to bless Thee, together with the Father and the Holy Spirit in one Godhead, and strength and power.

For Thou, O Christ, art the radiance of the Father, the

immutable, steadfast tracing of His being and His nature.
O Fountain of Wisdom, and fathomless source of Goodness,
open our heart and confirm our minds to know Thee,
the One True Son of God Who didst take upon Thyself
the sins of the world.

Stretch forth Thy hand to us who are tossed about in
this world as Thou didst to Peter sinking in the sea, and
with Thy strength fortify us against the devil that doth
contend with us. Feed us, with Thine ineffable wisdom
governing all creation. Kindly refuge for the storm-tossed,
the one true course, shew us the way, and therein will we
walk, for unto Thee have we delivered our souls. Bestow
on our foolishness Thy spirit of true understanding. Bless
our every work with the breath of Thy fear, that at all times
guided and sustained by Thy Holy Spirit we may in all
things work Thy holy and all-perfect will. Make us to be
servants of Thy New Testament which is in Thy Blood,
O Jesus our Saviour. Grant that we may be servants of Thy
holy mysteries. Of Thy great mercy accept us, that we
may be worthy to offer unto Thee a spiritual sacrifice for
our sins; and vouchsafe that without iniquity we may serve
Thee all the days of our life, that we also may receive the
reward of Thy faithful servants and wise workers in
the dread day of Thy righteous judgment.

For Thou dost know, O Christ, that we have no other
god save Thee, and unto Thee only, together with the
Father and the Holy Spirit, we offer worship and praise at
all times.

IX. ALMIGHTY LORD, Son of the Father without
beginning, and Word: O Jesus Christ, we pray Thee, of
Thine ineffable mercy in no wise to forsake Thy servants,
but remain in us always, and grant unto us the
imprescriptible joy of Thy salvation. Enlighten our mind
with the imperishable light of knowledge of Thee.
Embrace our souls with the love of Thy cross; and fill our
bodies with the fragrance of Thy purity. Cleanse us

throughly, and adorn us. And if Thou dost discern in us the way of iniquity, turn us aside, and stablish us on the path of Thy truth.

For Thou only art the way, the truth, and the life, and unto Thee we ascribe glory, together with the Father, and the Holy Spirit; now, and for ever: world without end. Amen.

X. O Holy and Merciful GOD, God eternal and all-good, Who hast promised to hear all them that in truth call upon Thee: Hear now our unworthy prayer, and come to save us from all them that oppress us. Forbid the unclean spirit from the face of our folly, and proscribe every spirit of enmity and rancour, of envy and flattery; the spirit of fear and despondency, the spirit of pride and anger. And may every passion kindled in us by the workings of the devil be extinguished in us.

Cleanse us from all filthiness of the flesh and spirit, and may our soul, our body and our spirit, be enlightened by the light of Thy divine knowledge, that by Thy manifold goodness all we, be it only in our old age, may attain to perfection of nature, in full measure, and thus being saved by Thy mercy, together with Thine angels and all Thy saints, we may glorify Thy great and glorious name, of the Father, and of the Son, and of the Holy Spirit; now, and for ever: world without end. Amen.

XI. O LORD JESUS CHRIST, Son of God and Word, Who in the searchless mystery of Thine incarnation didst make manifest to us the Father as light, in which there is no darkness at all: Send down Thy Holy Ghost upon us, as Thou didst upon Thy holy Apostles, that He may teach us to know Thee, and manifest us sons of Thy Light. We beseech Thee, hear and have mercy.

XII. O LORD, long-suffering and very gracious: Incline Thine ear to us, and attend to the voice of our supplications. Mark us with the token of Thy divine mercy, and by Thy Holy Spirit stablish us in Thy truth. Rejoice our hearts with the life-giving fear of Thy Holy Name. For great art Thou Who doest great wonders.

Thou alone art God, plenteous in mercy, and good in Thy strength, Who dost comfort and save all them that put their trust in Thee. Wherefore hear us now, lowly and condemned, and accept us who bow down and cry unto Thee: Remember not the sins of our youth, nor our ignorance, and cleanse us from secret faults. Cast us not off in the time of old age; forsake us not when our strength faileth. Leave us not even unto our last breath, but vouchsafe us ere then to come to Thee, and with understanding attain unto Thy high glory.

Yea, O most merciful Lord, look down from the height of Thy holy dwelling place on us who now stand before Thy face, and await Thy rich mercy. Visit us with Thy goodness. Deliver us from every assault of the devil, and confirm our life in Thy holy and sacred commandments. By the working of Thy Holy Spirit wash away all filth, and by Thy strength keep us all the days of our life; through the prayers of the most holy Mother of God and ever-Virgin Mary, of Thy holy and all-glorious Apostles and of all the saints that have been pleasing in Thy sight since time began. For Thou alone art God, and unto Thee we ascribe glory, unto the Father, and unto the Son, and unto the Holy Spirit.

ABSOLUTION

O ALMIGHTY GOD, our heavenly Father,
Whose desire is for each and every one to enter
   into the knowledge of thy truth,
We pray and beseech thee to grant salvation
   unto these thy servants.
Assuage their pain, O Lord.
Release them from the bondage of sin.
Forgive them their trespasses, voluntary and
   involuntary; whether freely confessed or
   unspoken through forgetfulness or shame.
For thou alone canst unbind what has been bound
   and make the crooked straight.
In thee, O Lord, is our hope and our expectation;
   for thou art merciful and everloving.
Grant therefore unto these thy servants
   forgiveness of sins and life everlasting;
Through the partaking of the precious Body
   and Blood of thy Christ.
In the Name of the Father, and of
   the Son, and of the Holy Ghost.

                                   Amen.

FOR THE CHAPEL

O LORD our God, whose might
upholdeth all creation:
Stablish the work of our helpless hands;
And make this lowly church
a place for the shewing of thy glory;
and for all peoples a house of prayer pleasing in thy
    sight.
We pray thee: Hear us and have mercy.

O LORD GOD of HOSTS, we beseech thee
that thine eyes may be opened
towards this house night and day:
That thou mayest hearken
when thy servants call upon thy holy Name;
And when thou hearest,
forgive and have mercy.

BEFORE THE CHERUBIC HYMN

I

O FATHER, SON, and SPIRIT,
Triune Godhead, One Being in three Persons,
Light unapproachable,
O Nature inviolable, Mystery most secret,
Who art hymned and worshipped by all creation,
Save us who honour Thee in faith and love.
We pray Thee, hear us and have mercy.

O ALMIGHTY GOD and our FATHER,
Fount of time and eternity,
Who by Thy power hast set a term to our life on earth,
and through Thine only-begotten Son dost grant unto us,
through resurrection immortal life
and a kingdom which cannot be moved –
accept us who implore Thee,
and sustain us by Thy Holy Spirit
as we approach Thy throne on high for bloodless
    ministration
and communion uncondemned in Thy Divine Mysteries,
We pray Thee, O Father all-holy, hear and have mercy.

LORD JESUS CHRIST, Everlasting King,
the only true High-Priest,
Who didst offer Thyself to God the Father upon the Cross
in atonement for the sins of the world,
and in this searchless act of service
didst give us Thine incorruptible Body for sacred food,
and Thy most precious Blood for life-giving drink –
Make us worthy of these ineffable mysteries,
That we may be partakers of the Divine Nature,
having escaped the corruption
that is in the world through lust,
We pray Thee, O Lord, hear and have mercy.

O HOLY SPIRIT, good Comforter, Giver of wisdom
and Light of revelation,
look down in Thy infinite mercy on the infirmities of our
nature;
be mindful of our sickness and our sorrows,
our labours and our tribulations,
and by Thy might enable us worthily to accomplish
this divine and solemn ministration,
We pray Thee, be swift to hear us and have mercy.

O GOD and FATHER without beginning,
Thou Who art blessed throughout all ages,
Who hast revealed unto us the mystery of a bloodless
ministration,
O Thou our great King – look down upon us
and deliver us from all that defileth flesh and spirit . . .
Illumine and hallow us,
that with a clean conscience and enlightened heart
we may share in Thy holy things,
and be united with Christ Himself,
our true God, Who said:
'He that eateth My Flesh, and drinketh My Blood,
dwelleth in Me and I in him' –
Renew our nature, by Thy word abiding in us,
and make us the temple of Thy Holy Spirit,

That being ever guarded by Thy might
we may give glory to Thee,
Father, Son and Holy Ghost,
now, and for ever: world without end.
Amen.

II

O FATHER all-good, O Only-begotten SON, O HOLY
  SPIRIT,
Life-creating TRINITY, Begetter of Light,
Who in Thine ineffable wisdom didst summon all creation,
visible and invisible, from non-being into being,
and by Thy might dost uphold all things;
Who according to Thy providence concerning mankind
hast given us this heavenly ministration –
Strengthen us by Thy grace to praise the majesty of this
  mystery
and with a pure heart and enlightened mind
to accomplish this holy sacrament in a worthy manner,
  We beseech Thee, hear us and have mercy.

O HOLY FATHER, Who art from all eternity and before
  all worlds,
Source everlasting of all that is,
Accept our prayer, Deliver us from the sorrow of sin,
Lift our minds to contemplation of Thine unfathomable
  judgments,
and fill our hearts with the light of Thy Divine Wisdom,
that we may serve Thee in spirit and truth even unto our
  last breath,
  We pray Thee, O Father all-holy, hear us and have mercy.

O LORD JESUS CHRIST, our God and Saviour,
Who art the one true Corner-stone and Foundation of
  every life,
Look down in mercy upon us, Thine unworthy servants,
who trust in Thy love,
and make bold to offer Thee our supplications and prayers,
and in Thy Blood wash away our every sin . . .
  We pray Thee, O Lord, hear us and have mercy.

O HOLY SPIRIT, Eternal King and Giver of life
  incorruptible,
Increase Thy mercy towards us
according to the multitude of our sorrows and our sighing,
and cast down every enemy that fighteth against us.
Do Thou Thyself work in us those things
which are pleasing in Thy sight,
and sanctify us with an imprescriptible hallowing of our
  souls and bodies,
  We beseech Thee, be swift to hear us and have mercy.

O GOD the FATHER Who art ever blessed,
Who hast called us to eternal glory in Jesus Christ,
Christ without sin, Who bore the sins of the world,
and laid His Life that we might live for ever;
Who in the weakness of human flesh
made manifest the image of Thy perfection –
We beseech Thee, Father all-holy,
fill us from on high with Thy strength,
that we may follow in His steps.
Make us like in goodness to Thy Son
in this proud, inconstant age,
that the way of Thy truth suffer no blasphemy
because of our untruth,
nor be profaned by the sons of the adversary.
Yea, Father all-holy,
of Thy goodness accept our ministration,
and make us worthy to partake
of the Body and Blood of Thy Christ,
and to be the habitation of Thy Spirit,

That being ever guarded by Thy might
we may give glory to Thee,
Father, Son and Holy Ghost,
now, and for ever: world without end.
Amen.

III

O HOLY TRINITY, our GOD, FATHER, WORD and
   SPIRIT,
one and single, triune Light,
Who by searchless command didst summon us
from the darkness of non-existence to this life,
and didst grant us to know Thee, the one true God —
vouchsafe that at this hour of our priestly service
we may bring unto Thee rightful thanksgiving,
   We pray Thee, hear us and have mercy.

ALMIGHTY GOD and our FATHER,
Who at that time didst pour out Thy Holy Spirit
on the Apostles and all who were with them,
and didst grant them to proclaim Thy greatness
in the tongues of every nation,
So now plentifully send down Thy Holy Spirit upon us,
Thine unworthy servants,
and through communion in the Divine Mysteries
of the Body and Blood of Thy Christ,
make us, who call upon Thy dread Name,
Children of Thy Light uncreated . . .
   We beseech Thee, O Father all-holy, hear us and have
   mercy.

O LORD JESUS CHRIST, Light everlasting,
Who from the Father didst shine forth before all worlds,
O Word (hypostatic) Who wast clothed in flesh,
and didst offer Thyself on the altar of the Cross
in sacrifice for our salvation —
Enable us worthily to partake of Thy holy mysteries,
that all that is of death in our flesh may be swept away
by Thine incorruptible Life,
   We beseech Thee, O Lord, hear us and have mercy.

O HOLY SPIRIT, mysterious Light;
O Light inscrutable, Light beyond all name –
Come and abide in us . . .
Deliver us from the darkness of ignorance,
and fill us with the stream of Thy knowledge;
raise us who are brought low in sin,
and vouchsafe that we may partake in the divine sacrament
of the incorruptible Body and Blood of Christ.
   We beseech Thee, be swift to hear us and have mercy.

O LORD JESUS CHRIST, Son of the living God,
Who didst open the eyes of the man that was blind from
   his birth,
Do Thou open the eyes of our hearts,
and grant us to behold Thee, our Creator and our God.
We beseech and implore Thee;
cast us not away from Thy presence –
and being not wroth with all our ungodliness,
our vileness and abomination,
Appear unto us, O Light of the world,
that we too may become sons and daughters
of Thine undying Light.
O loving Christ, Who didst send down from the Father
the holy Comforter to Thy disciples,
Grant, O Thou who art all good,
even unto us, the least of men,
the gift of Thy Holy Spirit to teach us to know Thee,
and to reveal unto us the mystery of the ways of Thy
   salvation.

That being ever guarded by Thy might
we may give glory to Thee,
with the Father and the Holy Ghost,
now, and for ever: world without end.
Amen.

IV

O HOLY TRINITY, FATHER, SON and SPIRIT,
The only Truth and God,
Ever-living and all-powerful,
Who art continually glorified in heaven and on earth,
make us worthy to abide unwavering in the Light of Thy
    commandment,
and deign to accept our praise and thanksgiving . . .
    We pray Thee, hear and have mercy.

ALMIGHTY and most merciful FATHER,
Send down Thy Holy Spirit to stablish us in the marvellous
    light of Thy will;
Heal our every infirmity;
Enfold our days in Thy care,
and make us steadfast in the confession of Thy truth
even unto our last breath . . .
    We pray Thee, O Father all-holy, hear and have mercy.

O LORD our SAVIOUR JESUS CHRIST,
The one true High-Priest,
Holy and undefiled,
cleanse us from all wiles and wickedness,
deliver us from the power of the evil one,
and lead us into the kingdom of Thy love,
that we, too, may be co-heirs with all the Saints
from the beginning of time
in this unfathomable mystery,
through the partaking of Thy divine Body and Blood,
    We pray Thee, O Lord, hear and have mercy.

O HOLY SPIRIT, All-powerful God,
Gracious Comforter and Almighty Defender,
Revealer of Truth
and strength that performest Sacraments –
at this holy present of the mystical Supper of Christ,
turn not Thy Face from us, who grieve Thee ever,
but Come and Condescend to our infirmities,
and, all things accomplished,
lead us, guiltless and without condemnation,
into His high chamber,
    We beseech Thee, be swift to hear us and have mercy.

O FATHER, the only good and holy,
Father of our Lord Jesus Christ,
Great God and Saviour of the World,
We beseech Thee, forsake us not;
but as in time of old
Thou didst send down Thy Holy Spirit
on the sacrifices offered by our fathers,
so now, of Thy goodness,
despise not our supplications, nor our worship,
but make us true servants of the New Testament,
which is in the Blood of Thy Christ.
Yea, Father, most Holy, account us worthy
to be the dwelling-place of Thy Holy Spirit,
and no longer an habitation of sin.
Send down into our hearts the fire of Thy Divine Love.
Come and Abide in us, with an eternal abiding,
together with Thine Only-begotten Son and Holy Spirit,

That being ever guarded by Thy might
we may give glory to Thee,
Father, Son and Holy Ghost,
now, and for ever: world without end.
Amen.

V

O HOLY TRINITY, consubstantial and undivided,
Most High God, King and Creator of all eternity,
Who hast honoured us with Thy Divine image,
and didst describe in the visible form of our nature
the likeness of Thine invisible Being —
Enable us to find mercy and grace in Thy sight,
that we may glorify Thee in the undying day of Thy
   Kingdom
with all Thy Saints throughout the ages,
with our fathers and forefathers,
with prophets and apostles,
with martyrs and confessors, with holy bishops and just
   men . . .
   We pray Thee, hear us and have mercy.

ALMIGHTY MASTER, GOD the FATHER,
the One Uncreated, Incomprehensible, Immutable,
Who didst give us in Thine Only-begotten and beloved
   Son
a pledge of our inheritance to come,   [daughters,
and didst show us the glory of being Thy sons and
Send down Thy Holy Spirit to work in us every good
   thing,
   We beseech Thee, O Father all-holy, hear and have
   mercy.

O LORD JESUS CHRIST, Author of Life,
Who dost uphold all things by the word of Thy might,
Who didst give Thyself as a ransom to death,
and cause life incorruptible to flow from Thy pierced side,
Turn not Thy Face from us, Thine unworthy servants,
but of Thy love toward mankind accept our humble service,
and pour out Thine abundant mercy on us
in this world and in Thy Kingdom to come . . .
   We beseech Thee, O Lord, hear and have mercy.

O HOLY SPIRIT, Heavenly King,
Boundless Source of Light, and plenteous Giver of Life,
Who alone dost give strength to the troubled
and upholdest the weak —
O Thou without Whom the strong shall weary
and the firm grow feeble,
Those who are full shall hunger, and young men shall
   bend —
Hear us in our affliction
and renew us by Thy strength,
and raise us to worthy service of Thee . . .
   We beseech Thee, be swift to hear us and have mercy.

O LORD JESUS CHRIST, Who art the brightness of the
   Father,
the express image of His Person,
the all-perfect tracing of His Essence and His Nature;
open our hearts and stablish our minds that we may know
   Thee,
the only-begotten and beloved Son of the Father,
Who dost take upon Thyself the sins of the world.
Behold, in fear and faith we stand before Thee,
resigning our despair to Thy deep mercy:
by the power of Thy Spirit raise us to follow in Thy steps,
Wash away our every sin, and cleanse us from all iniquity,
and make us worthy servants of the New Testament,
which is in Thy Blood, O Jesus our God.
Suffer us to offer unto Thee this holy sacrifice.

That being ever guarded by Thy might
we may give glory to Thee,
with the Father and the Holy Spirit,
now, and for ever: world without end.
Amen.

VI

O HOLY TRINITY, FATHER, WORD and SPIRIT,
One true God, Triune Light,
bottomless ocean of goodness and principle of all that exists,
Who commanded the light to shine out of darkness,
let the light of Thy knowledge shine forth in our darkened
    hearts,
and in the earthen vessels of our nature manifest Thine
    invincible strength
making us impervious to all evil.
    We pray Thee, hear us and have mercy.

O GOD the FATHER, Almighty and most Merciful,
Boundless Source of Light and fountain of Wisdom,
Diffuse over us the Light of Thy knowledge
and let nought that is unlawful be added to Thy truth,
which Thou hast revealed to us,
that our ministration before Thee
may be in all ways undefiled and holy,
    We pray Thee, O Father all-holy, hear us and have mercy.

O LORD JESUS CHRIST, eternal King of Glory,
The beloved Son and Word of the Father,
Who wast afterward clothed in flesh,
and didst offer Thyself on the altar of the Cross
as a sacrifice for our salvation –
accept us now who bow down before Thee,
and vouchsafe that we may be partakers
of Thy divine Body and Blood unto the healing
and hallowing of our souls and bodies . . .
    We pray Thee, O Lord, hear and have mercy.

O HOLY SPIRIT, consubstantial and glorified
together with the Father and the Son,
Almighty and all-powerful Lord,
Fount of life, Giver of Wisdom, and Light of Revelation,
Who by Thy descent didst bring the uttermost parts of the
    world
to the only true knowledge of God,
Do Thou Come down now even upon us,
who grieve Thee always,
to enlighten and sanctify us,
to heal and comfort us with Thine abiding comfort,
    We pray Thee, be swift to hear us and have mercy.

O FATHER ALMIGHTY, the only living and life-giving
    God,
from Whom every light of being doth proceed,
forsake us not
who have erred and strayed from Thy ways like lost sheep;
Yea, we have offended against Thy Fatherly love;
we have done those things
which we ought not to have done,
and we have left undone those things,
which we ought to have done.
Behold, in our despair we stand now before Thee
as miserable offenders,
and we implore Thee:
Restore our nature by the power of Thy Holy Spirit,
Illumine and hallow us by Thy Word abiding in us;
Stablish us in the likeness of Thy beloved Son,
that our hearts may be formed in His ineffable Image,
in which Thou didst fashion man . . .

That being ever guarded by Thy might,
we may (worthily) give glory to Thee,
Father, Son and Holy Ghost,
now, and for ever: world without end.
Amen.

IN THE END

O CHRIST our GOD,
Desire of our hearts,
Diffuse the light of Thy truth over us,
that in Thy light, unworthy as we are,
we may behold Thy glory
as of the only-begotten of the Father,
and so be fashioned after Thy searchless image,
in the likeness of which Thou didst create man.

O God our Saviour, light of our minds,
may Thy strength abide in us,
that we may ever be in Thee,
bearing always within us Thy Holy Spirit.

Grant us to know Thy love for mankind,
and make us like unto Thee, our Lord and our God,
as all Thy saints through ages were like unto Thee.

Yea, Lord Jesus Christ,
according to Thine unfailing promise
come and make Thine abode in us,
together with the Father and the Holy Spirit,
from everlasting to everlasting.

PRAYERS FOR DEPARTED SOULS

O ALMIGHTY GOD and our FATHER, fount of time
and eternity, who by Thy power hast set a term to our
life on earth, and through Thine only-begotten Son dost
grant unto us, through resurrection, immortal life and a
kingdom which cannot be moved, do Thou remember Thy
servant N. who hath fallen asleep in the hope of
resurrection unto life eternal,
 we beseech Thee, hear and have mercy.

O FATHER, holy and good, for as by the offence of one
man, our forefather, sin entered into the world, and death
by sin, so may we be inheritors of eternal life by the
righteousness of Thine all-perfect Son, and do Thou give
rest to the soul of Thy servant N. and preserve it unto the
blessed life that is with Thee,
 we beseech Thee, hear and have mercy.

O LORD GOD, FATHER ALMIGHTY, in the name of
Thy beloved Son, our hope,
Who gave Himself for a ransom to death wherein we
were held fast and continue so to this day, sold under sin:
Do Thou loose the grievous shackles of our death, make us
sons of resurrection, and receive into Thy rest, (where all
Thy saints have found repose) the soul of Thy servant N.
 we beseech Thee, hear and have mercy.

O LORD JESUS CHRIST, Eternal God, Who dost uphold all things by the power of Thy word, Who didst make Thyself of no reputation, and took upon Thee the form of a servant, wast crucified and descended into hell; Who opened the way of resurrection for all flesh slain by sin and in the bondage of corruption, give rest to the soul of Thy servant N. who hath set his hope in Thee, our Maker, the Author of our being, and our God,

we beseech Thee, hear and have mercy.

O LORD JESUS CHRIST, Who in the days of Thy sojourn with us in the flesh, and Thy saving passion didst cry unto Thy Father: Holy Father, I will that they also, whom Thou hast given me, be with me where I am; that they may behold my glory, which Thou hast given me: for Thou lovedst me before the foundation of the world: Mercifully now receive Thy servant N. who is come before Thee, and accept him as a partaker of Thine imperishable glory,

we beseech Thee, hear and have mercy.

For Thou art the resurrection and the life and the repose of Thy departed servant N. O Christ our God; and unto Thee we ascribe glory, together with Thine eternal Father, and Thy most holy, good and life-giving Spirit; now, and for ever: world without end. Amen.

May Christ our true God who is risen from the dead, by the prayers of his most holy Mother; of the holy and all-glorious apostles; of our righteous and holy fathers, and of all the saints; stablish in the mansions of the righteous the soul of his servant N. grant him rest in Abraham's bosom, and number him with the righteous, and upon us have mercy. For He is good and loving-kind.

FOR THE HOLY LITURGY

O THOU THAT ART,
O God the Father, Almighty Master,
before whom all creation bows down in praise:
Vouchsafe that we may worship and glorify Thee,
the one true God and our Father,
for the greatness of Thy love
with which Thou so loved us, unworthy as we are,
that Thou didst give Thine only-begotten Son,
that in Him and through Him we may become
sons and daughters of Thy light.

Enable us by Thy Holy Spirit at this dread hour
of the mystical supper of Christ
blamelessly to stand before Thine altar
and perform this reasonable and bloodless sacrifice
for our sins and for the sins of the whole world.

PRAYER AT THE BLESSING OF AN IKON OF CHRIST

O THOU THAT ART

God the Father, Almighty and proper to be worshipped, it is very meet, right and befitting the majesty of Thy holiness that we should praise and adore Thee, of certainty the One True God; Who art from everlasting, searchless, unknowable, ineffable.

Look down in mercy upon us and upon this ikon of Thine only-begotten Son, Who being the brightness of Thy glory and the express image of Thy Person, doth uphold all things by the word of His power; Who being God pre-eternal shewed Himself upon earth; being incarnate of the Holy Virgin emptied Himself and took upon Him the form of a servant in the likeness of our earthly body that He might mould us like unto His glorious body; giving Himself a ransom unto death, and having descended by the cross into hell, and being risen again the third day, ascending into heaven He sat on the right hand of Thy Majesty on high.

WHEREFORE, O Father all-holy, we have fashioned this image of Thy beloved Christ, and we pray and beseech Thee, of Thy goodness send down Thy Holy Spirit upon this ikon, to bless it and hallow it, that all who pray here may be heard of Thee and receive Thy heavenly blessing, and the grace of Thy Holy and life-giving Spirit, and the hallowing of Thine only-begotten Son.

For Thou art our sanctification, and to Thee we ascribe glory, now, and for ever: world without end. Amen.

> May this ikon of our Lord Jesus Christ
> be blessed and hallowed
> by the sprinkling of holy water
> In the Name of the Father
> and of the Holy Spirit.   Amen.